ALL YOU HAVE IS A VOICE

Free from a Hidden Cult

VICKI YOHE

Rekindled Flame
by MIGMIR Company

ALL YOU HAVE IS A VOICE
FREE FROM A HIDDEN CULT

Rekindled Flame Publishing House
an imprint of

MIGMIR Company USA, LLC

www.migmir.us

For Worldwide Distribution
Printed in the U.S.A.

ISBN: 9781952253003

Library of Congress Control Number: 2020932840

TABLE OF CONTENTS

ACKNOWLEDGMENTS

Thank you Jesus Christ for a second chance, I'm more in love with you than ever before. Thanks for the reminder that my sin is in the sea of forgetfulness.

For if the blood of bulls and of goats, and the ashes of an heifer sprinkling the unclean, sanctifieth to the purifying of the flesh: How much more shall the blood of Christ, who through the eternal Spirit offered himself without spot to God, purge your conscience from dead works to serve the living God?
—Hebrews 9:13-14

I dedicate this book to all the women from all over the world that Taylor has abused, physically, emotionally, mentally and sexually. I will continue to be your Voice. I will continue to sound the alarm, enough is enough.

I want to thank my family who stood with me through one of the darkest times of my life.
Hank and Amanda Dunkerson, you loved me back to life.

Joshua Yohe and your amazing wife Ashley, you both have been my rock.

Troy Hodges, thank you for caring for our boys and being there for me through every bad decision I have made.

My handsome sons, Walker and Adley, forgive me for not being there for you. I will make you proud of me again I promise.

Joni Lamb, for sending me for extensive counseling. You gave me hope that I would get through this. "Living Waters" brought life back to me.

Denise Boggs, thank you for reminding me about the stony heart. I will never be the same.

To the more than 100 women who reached out to me, please know that I love you and continue to walk in your true destiny.

My Australian friend Tanya West, you have been such a great friend. I'm grateful your eyes were opened, you are a gift from God to me, so special.

My Facebook family, thanks for standing with me, you all are the best.

Dr. Roy Etienne Smith and his wife EShawnna, thank you for all your hard work and believing in me.

Larry Reid, you have been a big part of exposing this wickedness. Thanks for speaking out against pimps in the pulpit. Thanks for your friendship and listening to my heart's cry.

Kedrick Scribner, the best security guy ever!!! How we met, only God could have connected us. Thank you for doing what you do in excellence and professionalism. You've always been there for me, love you.

ENDORSEMENTS

"I saw that my sister was hurt, wounded and bleeding. I reached out and sent her to a place for healing...God healed and restored her heart. Now, she tells her story with a clear voice so that others may hear the truth about control, manipulation and abuse."

—Joni Lamb, Daystar Television

"I'm so proud of my friend and colleague in ministry. She has come through her brokenness and now is walking in freedom! I personally know the amount of courage and bravery it takes to lay your issues out publicly for all to see, but when we humble ourselves, it is God who raises us up! Look at you girl!!! Keep running!"

—Pastor Hope Carpenter
Redemption Church, San Jose, CA

"Vicki Yohe has the heart of Jesus and He will not let any footsteps she has taken be wasted."
—Hank Dunkerson, Knob Lick, KY

"Grabbing her in my arms I felt in that moment as if she was my own sister. I wanted to help take her pain away." Love you Vicki, the future is so much brighter with your VOICE in it!"

—Amanda Dunkerson, Knob Lick, KY

"Anyone who has heard Vicki Yohe sing with that distinct and anointed voice can tell you she is the best friend a song could ever have. Vicki has been a great friend to me for many years and God has used her and continues to use her in my life and ministry. Her voice paints her love for Jesus, and as we listen, her song takes us all into the very presence of the Lord."

—*Darlene Bishop*
Solid Rock Church, Monroe, OH

"I have known Vicki for years and have loved her anointing, passion and desire to lead people to Jesus through worship. The cry of her heart has always been, "use me Lord" and that is exactly what He is doing, using her voice and story to bring light to secret darkness. This book will help give you the strength and courage to break free from abuse and control and live a life of complete freedom."

—*Pastor Robin Pruitt*
Faith Builders Church, Milwaukee, WI

"Vicki Yohe is a whole beast. She's like a bull dog for Jesus and people. She's an advocate for the voiceless, hurting and afraid. I've watched her go through hell and come out on fire. We were reconnected by a sad situation of betrayal, but she wasn't afraid and kept my heart strong and focused. Her words to me through the process were, "FEAR is a LIAR." She's proof you can have a voice and refuse to be bullied. Proud of her for writing this book. What looks like anger is really passion to end double standards in the name of God."

— *"Real Talk" Kim*

"When I first met Vicki she was so broken from the abuse she had suffered. Vicki, like many other women had trusted a man who said he loved her but in reality he loved himself.

Vicki needed a Safe Place where she could grieve and her heart healed from the pain of abuse and betrayal."

—*Denise Boggs, Living Waters Ministry*

FOREWORD

There is an area of life that has been plaguing mankind since the fall of humanity. We live with "it" every day and have just learned how to mask "it." We don't realize that the results of "it" have been catastrophic. We all have been its victim. And "it" has hindered us from being all of who we were created to be. We were created to be a reflection of God in the earth. "It" is the spirit of deception.

Deception is an act or statement which misleads, hides the truth, or promotes a belief, concept, or idea that is not true. In today's society, there are so many women (both inside and outside of the church) who are suffering silently in relationships, while living under the control of the spirit of deception. It takes real courage to come out from under that control and to tell the story so that others can be set free.

The enemy would love to silence women, especially the women of God. Nevertheless, as Vicki says, "All we have is a voice." God wants us to use our voice to be a witness to others— not becoming ignorant of the devil's devices. We are to know of God's saving grace through the Lord Jesus Christ!

May you experience the freedom and love of God in this book, "All You Have is a Voice" ~No More Secrets, by Vicki Yohe.

Apostle Cynthia Brazelton
Victory Christian Ministries International

INTRODUCTION

The ink generated from every step of a journey through life, writes a story every single day. Some days, the story is bright and fun— some days, dark and lonely.

Some parts of the journey are gloriously filled with power and promise. While others reek of painful inadequacies and failure. (We all experience it.) My lifelong friend, Vicki Yohe, has definitely walked it all.

Thankfully, in her story, you will see what is possible in all our stories,—how the ink can turn from ebony black to bright crimson. And when the blood of Jesus starts to write your story—His rich, royal red, redemptive pen of hope, can obliterate the cruelty of facts and failures, and rewrite what could have been a painful tragedy, into a beautiful story of triumph.

You've heard her song, now, hear her story. They both carry the banner of hope, and restoration, for all who are broken!

Geron Davis

Composer/Worship Artist

CHAPTER 1

HUMBLE BEGINNINGS

I had to be Born

DURING DELIVERY, JULY 13, 1965, the doctors didn't think I would make it. My Mom told me how they came into her room and she heard them saying, "We're going to lose the Mom." Then in another conversation they said, "We're going to lose the baby, lets save Mom." Then it shifted to they may lose both of us. My Mom cried out to the Lord, "Jesus, help me." She told me, "You had to be born!" Thank God I lived. Great is His faithfulness towards me.

I was born into a home that served the Lord. Dad was a preacher and I was the youngest of four. There were three of us girls and one boy. The church (U.P.C.)[1] was 70% African-American. I learned soul. I learned how to embrace all cultures and love all people; we are all children of God!

Sing Vicki Sing

Music was always a great part of my life. My father traveled as an Evangelist in his early years of ministry. My Dad, Mom, and her sister Gracie, had a trio who sang soulful, tight harmony with no music. They were very much in demand. I remember requesting to sing in church one Sunday night when I was only five years old. I wrote a note and sent it up to my Dad. I had written a little song called, "I don't wear no miniskirts; I believe in God." Dad said, "Vicki, your skirt is two inches above your knees. You can't sing that." I told him I had fifteen verses, and would just leave that verse out of the song. Funny however, I got to singing and forgot to leave that verse out and started tugging on my skirt to cover my knees. I've found that when I feel passionate about something, it becomes difficult just to "let it go." I am passionate about my relationship with God, my family, and yes my voice!

I grew up singing unto the Lord as far back as I can remember. When I was 12, my sweet

Mother made me realize that singers were a dime a dozen; any and everybody was singing it seemed. She said, "Vicki, be more than inspiring. Be anointed!" She always reminded me that it was the anointing that breaks the yoke. From what my Mom told me about the anointing, I wrote this song:

Here I am again Lord, Asking for more

Fill me up completely, With the anointing oil

Not only my head, But every part of me

I'm yielded and humbly thine, A servant to thee

Anoint me Lord this day, As I go along my way

Let my life send forth a glow, Let the oil around me flow

Anoint me Lord, This day I pray

Amen

Broken hearts and lives

Can be mended anew

Just with one touch

Dear Lord from you

Let the oil and the wine

Bring healing divine

To every wounded soul

Let it overflow

My Own Timeline

Many times we set our own timeline in our lives for what we think we want or is "supposed to happen." I was no different. I set timelines for when I thought I should be married. Where I should have been at a certain stage in my life, my goals, my success, everything! A lot of women think as I did, "I'm 30, I should have been married by now," or whatever age it is for some. I remember when I was just a teen, my Mother talked to us girls about our wedding day. She would tell us, "You don't want anyone snickering when you walk down the aisle in that white dress. You want to save yourself for your husband," which I did.

I was a virgin at 30 years old when I married my husband. Should I have? Should we have waited? Both questions are irrelevant as I made the decision to be married. I was married for 18 years. Even though I had experienced so much success in ministry, my marriage had failed, and ended in divorce. Most "Believers" who get divorced feel as though they let God down. There are whispers and silent questions by the church. Some feel broken, unloved, and have a need to "fit in" somewhere. I had hope that whatever was next for me, things would be better. I had no idea, things would get worse. Through it all however, I continued to witness the faithfulness of God; I am so grateful.

GREAT IS THY FAITHFULNESS[2]

Great is Thy faithfulness
O God my Father
There is no shadow of turning with Thee
Thou changest not
Thy compassions they fail not
As Thou hast been
Thou forever will be

Great is Thy faithfulness
Great is Thy faithfulness
Morning by morning new mercies I see
And all I have needed Thy hand hath provided
Great is Thy faithfulness
Lord unto me

Pardon for sin
And a peace that endureth
Thine own dear presence to cheer
And to guide
Strength for today
and bright hope for tomorrow
Blessings all mine, with ten thousand beside

For nothing is hidden that will not be made manifest, nor is anything secret that will not be known and come to light —*Luke 8:17 (ESV)*

USING YOUR VOICE

Your reflections from Chapter 1

_____

_____

_____

_____

_____

_____

_____

_____

_____

_____

_____

_____

CHAPTER 2

"OMG,
YOU'RE BEAUTIFUL!"

THE YEAR 2017 WAS a year that started with much reflection and turmoil.

Someone had sent me a meme of Jesus with luggage which read, "On my way back to the White House." I reposted it on my Instagram in support of President Trump. When I say "support," one cause that is dear to me is anti-abortion. As a woman who cannot birth children of her own, and have adopted children, I am an advocate of this cause. I associated the President with the upholding of some religious freedoms and traditional values I was brought up to honor and hold dear. Ironically "pro choice" is a woman's right to choose. I choose to support his efforts and campaign promises like any American who voted for one candidate or another over their life time. Nevertheless, I wasn't thinking about the impact it would have, or how it could be taken out of context from what I was truly feeling and trying to express. I was thinking about the Kingdom, not a political party or race. Right before I posted it, I saw two white women at the march with a sign that said, *"If Mary would have had an abortion, we wouldn't be in this mess."* (That broke my heart seeing such wickedness.) I apologized for not being sensitive to the state our country was in, and not realizing the meme would be offensive.

One thing about me, I have no problem admitting when I'm wrong—or there would have been no way I could have gone public with this story about being free from a hidden cult! Some didn't want to hear my side of the story; they just began calling me a racist, while others canceled ministry events with me. I was hurt. I was extremely saddened. I love people and hurting anyone was not my intent. I was broken and I didn't know how to fix it.

Then later that year, I got the call. I was asked to sing for a ministry event with David E. Taylor of Joshua Media Ministries International (J.M.M.I.)[3] I sang for the service during the first week of August. I was only to be at the crusade for one night. I was suppose to fly out the next morning at 7:00 A.M. Well, the service was still going at 3:30 A.M. (very cult-like, keeping your followers sleep deprived) I tried to change my flight, but there was no flight out until the following day. We contacted Michelle (David's assistant) to extend the room for one more night. I surprised him at his birthday party and sang a few songs. After the party, we took a selfie in the green room. He gave me his number and asked if I would text it to him.

At around midnight, I sent him the picture and thanked him for everything. He responded,

"OMG, you're beautiful!"

I said, "thank you."

Then he asked me, "Are you dating anyone?"

I responded, "Whoa nelly"

He said, "I'm a lion. I move fast.

I liked how that skirt fit tight on your body tonight!"

I responded, "I had gained some weight. I did not wear it tight intentionally." He continued to brag on my appearance. In past relationships I was told I was "cute" and your basic type of compliments. Even in my marriage, I don't recall ever being called "beautiful." It felt good to hear. A door was opened. Satan knows how to get you!

Now the serpent was more subtil than any beast of the field which the Lord God had made. And he said unto the woman, Yea, hath God said, Ye shall not eat of every tree of the garden? And the woman said unto the serpent, We may eat of the fruit of the trees of the garden: But of the fruit of the tree which is in the midst of the garden, God hath said, Ye shall not eat of it, neither shall ye touch it, lest ye die. And the serpent said unto the woman, Ye shall not surely die: For God doth know that in the day ye eat thereof, then your eyes shall be opened, and ye shall be as gods, knowing good and evil. And when the woman saw that the tree was good for food, and that it was pleasant to the eyes, and a tree to be desired to make one wise, she took of the fruit thereof, and did eat, and gave also unto her husband with her; and he did eat.

—Genesis 3:1-6

For days following that crusade, this man would face time me a couple of times and would text me saying, "I love you, or I love you babie." The "I love you" did seem strange, but I was open. Maybe this is the "one." At the end of August, I was asked to sing again at a crusade. I sang the first night at the crusade. Afterwards, someone on his staff text me saying, "Apostle wants to know where you are." I went back to my hotel and had gone to sleep.

It was the second night of the crusade when he asked to talk to me after the service. We sat in the lobby of the Ritz-Carlton for four hours. He looked at me and he said, "I was looking at you tonight and I can tell you right now your bra size." I was totally shocked that he was that comfortable speaking to me like that when we had never had a date. I started laughing and I said, "There is no way." He then told me my bra size. We continued talking and he wanted to hold my hand. He attempted to impress me with talks of stuff he had at his home, and I quickly did convey that all of those things did not impress me. As it neared 4:30 A.M., I said, "I need to go to my room. I need to go to the restroom." I decided to use the restroom in the lobby of the hotel. When I came out, he grabbed me, and he kisses me. I told him I had to go.

He then said, "Let me walk you to your room."

And I said, "There is just no way."

Well, we ended up at the door. After 30 minutes outside the door, of course he wants to come in. Scripture says, "Give no place to the Devil." Nevertheless, I did. He wanted to lay on the bed and talk.

He said,

"Don't worry; we will keep our clothes on."

I didn't even realize that I was being seduced. There I was, in a long, black dress. He had a suit on. What could go wrong? He said he was getting cold. We both got under the blanket. Things quickly escalated into sin. Do I put all the blame on him? Certainly not, I was wrong. Vicki Yohe made another bad decision.

"Wherefore putting away lying, speak every man truth with his neighbour: for we are members one of another. Be ye angry, and sin not: let not the sun go down upon your wrath: Neither give place to the devil."   *1 Peter 4:25-27*

USING YOUR VOICE

Your reflections from Chapter 2

_____

_____

_____

_____

_____

_____

_____

_____

_____

_____

_____

_____

_____

CHAPTER 3

UNDER THE INFLUENCE

SOME HAVE DECIDED TO judge me and say, "I thought you were a praise and worshipper." As I have said before, I'm as human as you are. I was looking for love and I thought I had found it. I was praying, but I wasn't watching. I eventually discovered that I was under the influence of a master manipulator. He almost destroyed my life. Manipulators mix the lie with a little bit of truth. He had the right scriptures, the right words, there was some faith in the room at the crusades—mainly because some of the people genuinely love and desire God. This is what made it so sick. There was so much twisting and deception of spiritual things. That's how they get you. You have pure motives and are focusing on what is true, but overlook what it's mixed with. This system empowers cult leaders each and every day. Therefore all "cult leaders" are extremely toxic and poisonous, like snakes.

David would say that Jesus was going to appear "physically" at his crusade. He would tell them what night etc. I noticed he attracted people who had a hunger to have a closer relationship with Jesus. Bragging that he had seen Jesus over 1,000 times and is His "best friend" pulls them in. Spring of 2017 I really wanted a closer relationship with the Lord myself and began praying and fasting. When I connected with J.M.M.I. in August and read the book "Face to Face," I thought this was a God thing. Knowing what I know now, I believe the whole book was made up and is full of lies. Lies are certainly what all cult leaders use to sustain their following. The lies sound so good and convincing that you can become intoxicated by them.

Jim Jones[4] poisoned his victims with a "special" drink. Dave Koresh used fear as his drink of choice. David E. Taylor and other abusers use a different type of "beverage," one much more discreet—one with a variety of flavors. The outcome is the same however, a type of death. Intoxication can be done by more ways than just alcohol or drugs. You can allow someone to have an intoxicating effect on you and your decisions. This can be accomplished mentally and emotionally, even financially at times. Symptoms are quite similar to those who are intoxicated by alcohol or drugs.

According to Center for Disease Control, there are seven stages of alcohol intoxication.[5]

1. (Sobriety or low-level intoxication)

"A person is sober or low-level intoxicated if they have consumed one or fewer alcoholic drinks per hour. At this stage, a person should feel like their normal self."

You just started drinking their "Kool-Aid." You have no idea anything is wrong. This is a "good person." "I am so glad to even be here," you may think. I was open to him and his ministry.

2. (Euphoria)

"A person will enter the euphoric stage of intoxication after consuming 2 to 3 drinks as a man or 1 to 2 drinks as a woman, in an hour. This is the tipsy stage. You might feel more confident and chatty. You might have a slower reaction time and lowered inhibitions."

Now it's starting to get good to you. You like what you see, you like what you hear. Your discernment has been lowered. I wanted God more than anything.

3. (Excitement)

"At this stage, a man might have consumed 3 to 5 drinks, and a woman 2 to 4 drinks, in an hour: You might become emotionally unstable and get easily excited or saddened. You might lose your coordination and have trouble making judgment calls and remembering things. You might have blurry vision and lose your balance. You may also feel tired or drowsy. At this stage, you are "drunk.""

You have now crossed the line, and have had "too much" of their crap to drink! I believed he was a true Man of God. I felt the ministry loved and accepted me.

4. (Confusion)

"Consuming more than 5 drinks per hour for a man or more than 4 drinks per hour for a woman can lead to the confusion stage of intoxication: You might have emotional outbursts and a major loss of coordination. It might be hard to stand and walk. You may be very confused about what's going on. You

might "black out" without losing consciousness, or fade in and out of consciousness. You may not be able to feel pain, which puts you at risk of injury."

You are confused. You can't tell the truth from a lie. The lines are completely blurry. You can't feel the pain of the abuse or the manipulation and dominance. I am in sin with the man, but kept justifying it as he provided justifications that were so far from the Word of God.

5. (Stupor)

"At this stage, you will no longer respond to what's happening around or to you. You won't be able to stand or walk. You may also pass out or lose control of your bodily functions. You may have seizures and blue-tinged or pale skin. You will not be able to breathe normally, and your gag reflex won't work correctly. This can be dangerous—even fatal—if you choke on your vomit or become critically injured. These are signs that you need immediate medical attention".

You are in deep. You have lost all control. Your boundaries are no longer an issue at all!

6. (Coma)

"Your body functions will slow so much that you will fall into a coma, putting you at risk of death. Emergency medical attention is critical at this stage."

At this point, you are a walking zombie with everything and everybody. You can't function or pray sometimes. You don't want to leave the house. You are near an emotional or mental death.

7. (Death)

You've allowed them to destroy everything you worked so hard for in your life.

I'm not perfect at all. I was vulnerable. I wanted to please him so much. He has pictures of me that are not appropriate. David expressed that he needed these pictures because we lived so far apart. He made me feel (in fear) as though I needed to send them in order to keep him; we rarely saw each other. I thought this was the man who I was going to marry one day and spend the rest of life with. I was not thinking nor being sober minder as scripture tells us to be as Believers.

Humble yourselves therefore under the mighty hand of God, that He may exalt you in due time: Casting all your care upon Him; for He careth for you. Be sober, be vigilant; because your adversary the devil, as a roaring lion, walketh about, seeking whom he may: Whom resist stedfast in the faith, knowing that the same afflictions are accomplished in your brethren that are in the world. But the God of all grace, who hath called us unto His eternal glory by Christ Jesus, after that ye have suffered a while, make you perfect, stablish, strengthen, settle you. To Him be glory and dominion for ever and ever. Amen. —I Peter 5:6-11

Things can be so broken inside that you don't even realize how bound you were until you really get free. David had my mind. One day I told him that once we were married, I would no longer travel and sing. I would just be with him and promote him and his ministry. He was for that 100%. He loves when it's "all about him."

"Pride goeth before destruction, and an haughty spirit before a fall." —*Proverbs 16:18*

USING YOUR VOICE

Your reflections from Chapter 3

CHAPTER 4

RED FLAGS, RED FLAGS!

I N THIS RELATIONSHIP, THERE was a lot of crying. There were many times, in the middle of the night, I found myself weeping. I would call his phone and leave a long message. David would never return the call and never acknowledged that I called. Many of the women who reached out to me told me the same thing. No matter how long they had been with him, some for just a year, others four, and five years; that they spent so much time crying.

I would get a text message from him every day, even though I didn't talk to him but once a month. That daily text helped me. Looking back now, it just doesn't make sense that someone who is in love with you would only find the time to talk to you once a month. I would ask him why can't we talk more often and he would rebuke me and say that I was unstable, and he couldn't be with an unstable woman. I would tell him I was sorry and I would try to understand. He would tell me he's busy in ministry traveling, and I needed to understand why he couldn't call as often as I wanted him to.

He had my mind. I would talk myself out of any red flags I would have. There were many red flags in the relationship.

November 2017 Thanksgiving David told me he would come to spend Thanksgiving with me and my boys at my sister's house in Nashville. Looking back now, I know he was just saying that and had no intentions of coming. David would tell you what you want to hear at that moment, but seldom would follow through. My boys were anxious to meet him, as were the rest of my family. The plan was for him to spend Thanksgiving with his parents in Memphis, then drive over to Nashville that day to spend the evening and the next day with us.

He sent a text message to me the day

before and said while he was boarding the plane he had a check in his spirit not to get on the plane and to cancel all the plans. He said Daniel had already started driving the Rolls Royce to Memphis. He had just made a call to tell him to turn around and come back to St. Louis.

I thought this was all legit and that he was hearing from God not to make the trip at that moment. But knowing what I know now, he would have never come and spent that time with my family. Think about it. It would have messed up his whole wicked scheme. My family would have taken pictures and posted them on Facebook. Then, the secret would have been out that he and I were together. That would have exposed him—all the other women who he told to be silent about their relationship would have found out. I just believed everything he said; I was under his mind control.

I remember asking David one day while lying in the bed with him, "Isn't this Wrong?" He ignored the question for a moment. Then he said, "I repent every day." He told me, "God understands this is my weakness." I knew in my heart that this wasn't right.

I was scheduled to sing at the crusade in December 2017. I knew we were "a secret." However, because I was the guest singer, it didn't seem awkward for me to be in his office.

When I first got there, I went straight to his office and I sat on the couch. I was going to wait until he got there because I hadn't seen him in a few months. I wanted to see him. I missed him.

We had been dating since August 2017. Again, hardly anyone knew about our "secret." David told me who knew about our relationship at different times, He said, "My son knows about us. My parents, Bishop George Scott and of course Michelle, Daniel and Marcia know." I asked about certain other leaders including one Prophetess. He told me, "No, they haven't been processed yet." After I exposed him, I texted this particular Prophetess to tell her I had been praying for her. I also shared that God clearly showed me all the so-called rumors about her and David were in fact true. Her response was, "I don't care if Apostle slept with 300 women and told them they would be his wife. I know what God told me."

Now sitting in his office with gifts I had brought to the crusade, I asked someone to get his son because I had a gift for him. His son came into the office, and I handed him a gift card. I asked him if he knew his Dad and I were dating. I felt sorry for him. He looked shocked. It was a very awkward moment. He said, "No he didn't know."

A few minutes later, Michelle walks in the

room. She gives me my Christmas gift from David—which I found very weird because I didn't know why David didn't give it to me himself. It was a black and gold Coach purse. She showed me the inside plate that she had made by his request. It said, "All my love."

When Marcia saw me in his office, she asked if I had permission to be in there.

I said, "He is my boyfriend and I am going to wait for him. He will not mind."

"Well, did he text you and tell you to wait on him here?" she asked.

I said, "No, but it's fine. I know he will want to see me."

By this time, I was in tears. So, I got up and left and went on the front row where I was supposed to sit for the crusade.

I sat there and texted David and I told him how rude she was. He never saw the text message until after the service. He told me she was totally out of line and she would be corrected. [Before the service started, she had come back to me and said I could go back to his office that she misspoke. I said, "It's okay. I'm perfectly fine here."] I stayed a few extra days to be with him. He sent me home with a $500 gaming console for my boys for Christmas.

Meryl Streep[6] once referred to prominent Hollywood film producer, Harvey Weinstein[7] as "God." Although she was making a joke at the time, she had no idea someone she trusted and appeared to be legit was involved in so many scandalous things against women behind the scene. Once his abuse of power came to light and all the women begin to speak up, she was ashamed and horrified. "When you are a trusting and caring person, sometimes you just get it wrong." [She said.]

USING YOUR *Voice*

Your reflections from *Chapter* 4

_____

_____

_____

_____

_____

_____

_____

_____

_____

_____

_____

_____

FINDING MY VOICE

WHEN YOU FIND YOUR voice, it is a sobering experience.

"Cry aloud, spare not, lift up thy voice like a trumpet, and shew my people their transgression, and the house of Jacob their sins."

—*Isaiah 58:1*

In July of 2018, I drove to St. Louis to spend time with David. I brought my boys. We stayed in his home in Chesterfield. The home was impressive. However, I noticed very quickly it was not homey. There were picture frames with no pictures in them. It was very cold. He took me to my room upstairs. He asked if I liked the bedroom set he picked "just for me." I know now that he told all the women (who he was deceiving and lying to) the same thing. I overheard him asking my youngest son, Adley, if he would like to live there.

One night David and I were in the theater room watching a movie. He was on his phone texting nonstop. I just slipped out, went to my room, and cried most of the night. The next day he never mentioned it. I know now he was texting women.

In October of 2018 we were in Israel for a crusade. While on the bus headed to the Wailing Wall[8], Michelle says, "Apostle wants Marcia and me to meet with you." I responded, "It's okay, he's my boyfriend. He can talk or text me directly." Her response was, "Apostle said, 'If you don't receive us, you don't receive him'." I agreed to meet with them. His staff decided to meet with me to "rebuke" me for trivial things. For one hour and a half, I sat in a chair and I cried. I guess they were "breaking me down." Telling me, literally that I wasn't worth anything.

In this meeting they told me that David would never announce me as his wife if I kept acting like a "diva." I've been traveling for 30 years and have never been accused of this. I wanted to defend myself. (That's pride) I kept thinking how could the man who loves me and says he's in love with me put me in a room with two women who were trying to break me down for an hour and a half? Who would do this to a person? I couldn't feel any love. It seemed wicked. It was evil.

They falsely accused me of things I did not do. When I would try to speak, Michelle would tell me to shut up! After they were finished, I walked out. As I was leaving, Marcia turned to me and said, ***"All you have is a voice."*** Do you know how brainwashed I really was? When I left the room, I actually sent David a text and thanked him for it. I tried to accept everything they were saying to me. I wanted and needed to please him. Little did I know, Marcia was speaking Prophetically. I am the voice of hundreds of women!

After I returned from Israel, a woman inboxed me. She said she knew I was connected with J.M.M.I. and had been introduced to David through my Facebook page. She then said, "I have been having an affair with him for 13 months." She sent me screen shots of texts from him. I literally froze reading them. My only response to her was, "You need to contact Michelle his assistant." I immediately sent David a text to call me. I got no response. I sent the screen shots to Michelle. She responded, "Have you reached out to Apostle?" I then called Daniel who was almost home. He said he would have David call me. I blew up David's phone with this woman's text messages—telling him you are texting her the same things you text me. He called with Michelle on the line. She's in on all his stuff. She helps him with the treachery. They wine and dine the rich people. I believe she plays a vital part in this whole thing.

"This is a movement. It is not okay to treat woman like this."

So he says,

"What's going on? I just woke up."

I proceeded to tell him about a woman who inboxed me on Facebook. He said,

"Block and delete her. She is a traitor."

I said, "But the pictures she sent were pictures of you in Israel just a few weeks ago."

He said, "Michelle, explain to Vicki."

"Vicki, Apostle gets a lot of women coming at him like this." she said.

I was so under his mind control, I dismissed the facts this woman gave and blocked and deleted her. I was still troubled, but I still wanted to believe that he was telling me the truth. A few weeks later, I was awakened at three o'clock in the morning by a voice that said, "Focus on the greater purpose of this relationship." At the time, I thought it was the voice of the Lord. I thought I had a "visitation" by Him. But now I know, it was demonic.

David interpreted it for me. He said, "I wasn't to question him about women. I was to trust him; he was faithful to me." I tried to move on from this, but it made me physically sick. I cried myself to sleep every night.

As the 2018 holidays were approaching just a few months ahead, I'm planning and asking about Christmas. He says, "Well, you know it's the most romantic time of year we'll get together." I say my boys are going to be with their Dad I'll be by myself. I'm just going to come on up to where you are. I'll be there with you. There was no answer from him at all. I later told him I would not be coming to the "one night with the king event." They cancelled my plane ticket. The Holy Spirit spoke to me to unblock that woman and ask her when she talked to David last. She sent me screen shots of him asking her for help with his new book. He said "hey wifey." The same phrase he would say to me.

Then someone else calls me on Messenger that used to go to the ministry. They told me they were told to block me. I said listen, "I've been dating Apostle since last August." "No you haven't," he tells me. "I know his girlfriend. They have been together for 7 years." I asked for her name and inboxed her. I had no idea that throughout my exposure of him, it turns out there are almost 100 women he has done and is doing this to. Women call me from

Israel and Holland. He's got women from London England, women from Australia and from all over the United States. They all think they're going to be his wife. I feel so bad because one woman went to his ministry because of me being on Facebook promoting him. He used my platform to advance his mess. I am now using it to expose it. I'm not the only one speaking up. God has given me a platform. This is a movement. It is not okay to treat women like this.

Remember Esther

Our dear sister Esther is mentioned more times in scripture than any of the other woman in the Bible. Esther was a woman of great faith. She had courage; she had heart. When she made the choice to expose the plot to destroy her and her people, she put her own life on the line.

For if thou altogether holdest thy peace at this time, then shall there enlargement and deliverance arise to the Jews from another place;but thou and thy father's house shall be destroyed: and who knoweth whether thou art come to the kingdom for such a time as this? Then Esther bade them return Mordecai this answer, Go, gather together all the Jews that are present in Shushan, and fast ye for me, and neither eat nor drink three days, night or day: also and my maidens will fast likewise; and so will I go in unto the king, which is not according to the law: and if I perish, I perish.
—Esther 4:14-16

I knew what was at stake for me to go public. Nevertheless, when I did, it freed me. It changed me. I could have walked away quietly, or been silenced with money or threats. But at the cost of losing it all, I chose to use my voice. Yes, Esther knew the consequences of her action, but the lives of her people mattered more. She opened her mouth and told who was behind the evil, "Haman!"[9]

Thank God she had the support of her cousin Mordecai. His wise counsel aided her success in standing firm, in standing strong. My own cousin Hank spoke similar words of comfort and challenged me to stand.

"Vicki came to our home in Kentucky, January of 2019, after going through the biggest battle for her soul. She was involved with a cult. We were shocked. Our hearts broke as she cried and shared what had happened and that many people wanted nothing to do with her because of her fall... We spent the next few months exposing the cult by way of the internet and live protest. Every day was filled with new worship to the Father. We watched God's light and love begin to flow back through the one He anointed and called." —Hank

A pastor's wife once said she learned valuable lessons from Esther's story:

1. God uses ordinary people.

2. She did not allow her difficult circumstances make her bitter.

3. Her beauty did not make her prideful.

4. God is Sovereign over the heart of the King.

5. She needed older mentors.

6. To be courageous was not her first response to God's Call.

7. She knew where to find her strength.

8. She waited on God's timing.

9. She loved her people more than her own life.

10. Her Influence lives on.

One thing that is valuable for me: Esther was a voice to those who had no voice. She was a voice to those whose voice had been silenced. Could you imagine what could have been the outcome had she let fear shut her up?

"Red Bottoms" Those ain't going back

David gave me gifts. I believe he did this because I was pushing him and his movement. I was bringing him creditability. I used my influence to get well-known speakers to his crusade who never heard of him before. One of my gifts was a pair of shoes valued at almost $1,000.00. Sometimes women are distracted by what they are getting from toxic men, but the whole time he is stealing from them things that matter most in life.

Then said Jesus unto them again, verily, verily, I say unto you, I am the door of the sheep. All that ever came before Me are thieves and robbers: but the sheep did not hear them. I am the door: by Me if any man enter in, he shall be saved, and shall go in and out, and find pasture. The thief cometh not, but for to steal, and to kill, and to destroy: I Am come that they might have life,and that they might have it more abundantly. —John 10:7-15

When most think about "Red Bottoms" they think about a very expensive pair of shoes by designer Christian Louboutin[10]. Indeed, Red Bottom shoes were one of the gifts given to me during my time with David. In fact, I got those before I first went public with my story. I had never had a pair of Red Bottoms. Nevertheless, the shoes represent more than fashion, more than a gift. They represent value. I have suffered so much loss as a result of this man, his ministry, and madness. There were times I felt worthless. However, I left with something much better, much brighter. I left with ME! The shoes speak "Vicki, you have value! Your mind is priceless. Your future is promising. Your voice is precious"—things that were held in bondage during the "relationship." No, those ain't going back!

"...and who knoweth whether thou art come to the kingdom for such a time as this?"

—Esther 4:14

USING YOUR VOICE

Your reflections from Chapter 5

_____

_____

_____

_____

_____

_____

_____

_____

_____

_____

_____

_____

CHAPTER 6

NO MORE SECRETS

"…But in order to be strong, you have to love yourself, and in order to love yourself, you need thorough self-knowledge, you need to know everything about yourself, including your most hidden secrets, the ones most difficult to accept."

—*Susanna Tamaro*

WHEN IT CAME TO secrets, I had experience in keeping secrets. When I was a small child, I suffered abuse at the hands of a family member and my Mom told me not to tell my Dad.

When I met David, I had social media issues and thought the whole

"...church people can be so messy."

private and secret thing was a good idea at the time. I would not have to deal with everything that came from a public relationship. He reminded me how church people could be so messy. So we kept things private. I really thought I had found my true soul mate. I told him up-front I can't be in a relationship that's not going in the direction of marriage. My kids would be involved, and I would need 100% commitment in any relationship I was in.

"Wonderful David." You had to tell him how wonderful he was to stroke his ego. Within your first 30 days, he gets inappropriate pictures of you. (All the women would tell you the same thing.) He planned to use these pictures if you ever told on him. This was one of his scare tactics to keep the women silent.

He comes to women for different reasons. David desired my social media platform of 1.4 million followers. From the moment David and I were together, he wanted me to get him into churches and on Christian television. It was always about money and how to make his movement bigger. Regretfully, I lost good friends introducing them to David Taylor. One Pastor continued to book him for meetings even after I exposed him. He didn't seem to care what David was involved in, even though I shared how David and I were in the same hotel and bed the first time David preached for him. Wow, he was still okay with having David speak. I'm sure you can figure out why.

Can two walk together, except they be agreed? —Amos 3:3

Every con artist seeks some sort of credibility to be effective at their con. David took pictures with Pastor Benny Hinn then lied saying Benny Hinn was his "spiritual father." When women from overseas went to his website and saw reputable ministries mentioned, like Benny Hinn and others it brought credibility to his scam. When Benny Hinn was asked about David Taylor, he said he didn't know the guy.

I've had to rethink everything David has told me. Looking back, I believe 99% of the things he told me were not true. He told me that one time he drove past a hospital and began to pray. He said everyone was healed and they shut the hospital down. He also told me that the Lord appeared to him to go next-door to the owner of the office building. "Tell him if he gives you the building, the next day he will get a billion dollars," God said. David said the man gave them the building because he got the money the next day. Lies, all lies!

I thought I was his "one and only." I read his book. I wanted a closer relationship with

God. I had a desire to see Jesus face-to-face. I did have an experience. I got caught up in the hype and wanted to believe I saw Jesus. Some when they reportedly have such encounters, they see a high angel, others a demon who has transformed into an "angel of light." I have encounters with God in worship and see Him in operation in my everyday life. My experiences are real regardless of a book, a movement, or someone else's claim. I saw what was "Jesus" to me at the time. In retrospect, I could be wrong. I saw Him or a representative of Him. David mixes biblical truths with his lies and con to win over people. Everything taught by cults is not a lie, but a distortion of the truth which is sometimes more dangerous than a bold face lie.

Miracle scams/Social media fraud

It has been reported in various places, and I know first-hand, that there are bogus miracles scams. From the purchasing of wheelchairs for the crusades to make it look like dozens were getting healed, to social media scams, and so much more.

One woman wrote me and said,

"I was on Facebook and came across a revival type

of program, and it was very interesting. As soon as I liked it, someone was in my messenger asking am I saved and then later for a donation of $100. As I watched, David Taylor had a woman singing I commented in the live feed,

'God Bless her but she is NOT My dear sister Vicki Yohe and I left it alone. The next day I received a message about being saved and David said (or someone representing him) that Vicki Yohe is a personal friend of his'

They said Vicki will be in concert and with a donation, you'll get all her CDs and a Book about her. I asked what amount the donation was, and he said the donation was to help get her to his church as well. It was $700." She got ripped off of course.

One of the women who came forth had only been saved for six months when David inboxed her and told her she was to be his wife as well. She was with him for 18 months. Mostly just sex texting, and when she would come to the crusade, Michelle would call her back to his office and he would put his hand up her dress to do inappropriate things. A few minutes later, he would go to the platform and act all "humble and holy."

I remember him telling me we could not sexually be together during the crusades because he had to focus on the meetings. However, since I exposed him all the women are talking. They enlighten me and told me they spent time with him during the crusade. If you ever wondered why he's always late, sometimes he's up to three hours late, it's because he is with women. One lady told me she slipped out of the hotel room while he was asleep. The service had already been going on for over an hour and a half.

So, the reason why he told me he couldn't be with me during the crusade is because he had many, many women he had to juggle.

Immediately after David would leave the platform, I would get a text message from him during the crusades or any meeting within seconds. He told me how beautiful I was and what I had on was hot. After the service, I would go back into his office. I would sit down at the table where they served food. David would be on the couch texting. Now I know who he was texting. He was texting all those women who were sitting around me including all his "spiritual daughters," some of whom he sleeps with. He tells them how beautiful they were. At that time, I just thought he might be dealing with some future engagements, or simply checking on his parents. I had no idea I was one in his harem of women.

I remember telling him, "There are so many beautiful women here. I know they all want you. They all want to be your wife." He would look at me and with such a passion say, "Look at you. None of them can compare to you." He would tell me, "I have loved before, but I've never been in love until I met you."

There are video after video and story after story all across the internet calling him a sexual predator and a crook. I am not a woman scorned or crazy. There are dozens of stories and plenty of proof before I said a word to anybody. If it were just a couple of women, I wouldn't be speaking, but all of these—100 and more women. He claims he repents. However, repent doesn't mean repeat!

Another woman emailed me this:

"...educate yourself on the dangers of destructive cults. Real life is truly stranger than Fiction and to quote Larry Lunceford, who also exposes David on YouTube, 'I can't make this stuff up'. As a mother with an adult child in David's Cult there are some truths people should be aware of [Allegedly] Child Protective Services had to protect David's own daughter from him because of physical abuse. (Thank you Rick Frazier for the deposition videos) David manipulated his own son to threaten his mother with revenge porn and then David purposefully released the images. David has J.M.M.I. members work long hours every day for zero dollars. Each cult member is responsible for meeting their daily $500 quota selling God's

good grace and David's books and tapes over the 24 hour prayer line.

Meanwhile David gloats over his swollen Kingdom of modern day slaves, mansions, luxury cars, expensive clothes, etc. All the while the taxpayer supports the cult members via EBT cards, Medicaid and housing for females with young children.

David claims he is a faith healer and a miracle worker. There is zero proof of one faith healing with a person's name and medical verification. Zero proof of Grandiose claims to control the sun and the moon, and my personal favorite David's ability to catch live bullets in his mouth. David claims he is Jesus' best friend and End time 5 Star General with his own Joel Army. Both of these claims are against the Word of God."

David claims he has 18 million in his movement and 359,000 churches under him. This is a lie of course. His leadership tells the followers that 189 countries are watching live during his meetings. However, there are only 25 watching on Facebook and 12 watching on Periscope.

Today, J.M.M.I. sees me as a traitor. His assistant sent me a threat calling me a snake, liar and idiot. In her threat, she said, "I challenge you to pursue harder." Oh yes, I certainly will!

USING YOUR $\mathscr{V}$OICE

Your reflections from $\mathscr{C}$hapter 6

_____

_____

_____

_____

_____

_____

_____

_____

_____

_____

_____

_____

BIGGER THAN ME

A S I HAVE SAID SO many times before, if this was just happening to "poor old Vicki," you probably would not be reading a book by me at this time. Yes, many others have come to similar conclusions about the J.M.M.I. "Cult" Cult? I wasn't the first person to call it that. I use to defend the ministry when people would say such things. I didn't see it. I wouldn't allow myself to believe it. There is just no way, someone would be doing these things to people. This "Apostle" was abusing their money, crushing their dreams and visions.

He is hurting women. He is harming the children of God. This "Preacher, 'Prophet,' and Predator" is polluting the Gospel and bringing confusion to his "follower's" walk with God. Everything with this guy is grand and big. Wait a minute—*not everything.*

His own insecurities demand him to appear greater than what he really is. In fact, he is very small. (In every way) He claims ministry associations that simply are not real, supporters and followers that do not exist, and power he does not possess. He literally "buys" relationships to boost his ego, which is the biggest thing he has.

David wants to be famous. His assistant wears a security earpiece that is not connected to anything. He wants those who come in contact with him to think he needs "security" because of his fame. His cravings for more power, more women, more sex, more money, more loyalty, and more fame drive him 120 miles per hour every day. David will crash. David will feel the burn. As more people are talking, more women are coming forward, and more exposure coming from God.

Naïve church people love to say, "Just pray for him." They fail to understand what stage of the game we are at with this.

Moreover if thy brother shall trespass against thee, go and tell him his fault between thee and him alone: if he shall hear thee, thou hast gained thy brother. But if he will not hear thee, then take with thee one or two more, that in the mouth of two or three witnesses every word may be established. And if he shall neglect to hear them, tell it unto the church: but if he neglects to hear the church, let him be unto thee as a heathen man and a publican.   —Matthew 18:15-17

David Taylor has received prayer. Many have warned him and showed him the love of God. However, he will not repent. He will not submit to any type of authority. He is heading for destruction. One of the women who reached out to me expressed this:

"When my husband and I were introduced to J.M.M.I., we believed all the hype and eventually were going to relocate to be hands on with the ministry. A chain of events began to happen that made me realize that something was not right. The deeper we got involved my husband began to change towards me! He began to treat me like I was an enemy if I questioned certain moves of ministry that bothered my spirit. He would literally tell them everything that I felt was a red flag. At this point I felt that they were controlling him, so I personally reached out to David E. Taylor via Facebook Messenger after being denied his contact number.

Even though I was respectful in my approach merely asking valid questions, I was met with a barrage of insults being called

Jezebel and stupid amongst other things. They even told me that my husband should leave me because I was the controlling one! I say "they" because I eventually found out from former members who left that there were three people replying to me from his account.

Being mistreated, verbally, by this ministry was not enough to convince my now ex-husband that these people were not real ministers. He agreed with everything they said and at that point I knew he was in deep. From that point on, the fighting between us became too much and David Taylor convinced my husband to leave me. David told him that Satan entered my heart and his destiny was now there with J.M.M.I.

My husband took his first paycheck that he got from a new job he started just a week prior and left me. He would try to reach out in emails still trying to convince me to come out to St. Louis but I told him there was no way I would be a part of a ministry that spoke to their people in the way they did me. Nothing I said, or his parents (who are both preachers) could convince him that what he was involved in was diabolical. A year later with the support of my family and friends I ended up filing for divorce."
– Ruth

Her story was so disturbing. This man

is breaking up marriages and using spiritual witchcraft and mind control. God is a God of order. God hates division.

A naughty person, a wicked man, walketh with a froward mouth.He winketh with his eyes, he speaketh with his feet, he teacheth with his fingers; Frowardness is in his heart, he deviseth mischief continually; he soweth discord. Therefore shall his calamity come suddenly; suddenly shall he be broken without remedy.These six things doth the LORD hate:yea, seven are an abomination unto him: A proud look, a lying tongue, and hands that shed innocent blood An heart that deviseth wicked imaginations feet that be swift in running to mischief, A false witness that speaketh lies, and he that soweth discord among brethren. —Proverbs 6:12-19

I received an email from this precious woman. Here is her personal experience:

"I am one of many women victimized by the deception of David E. Taylor. I first met him when he came to my, now ex-husband's, church. Shortly after, he approached me on Facebook Messenger and I communicated with him because he was so understanding of my separation with my husband, but then he became sexual very quickly. It was both unexpected and strange, but at the time I was very vulnerable and he started to proclaim his love for me. He really started portraying a love for me that I did not have before—so I got hooked.

I had been dealing a lot with religious people at that time so when it became sexual,

I knew it was wrong but it's like it didn't matter because I wanted love. He made me believe we would be married and it was all okay…He swore me to silence. I could not tell anyone. He always said not now and the relationship went on for four years.

In the end, I found that David E. Taylor had been telling many women the same things he had told me and was having sex with them—even destroying marriages. I was suffering spiritually, emotionally, and even physically. I could only pray for Jesus to rescue me. It all happened after Vicki Yohe was courageous enough to come out publicly to tell her story, which is so very similar to many, many others. So much more has been found out about the fraud this man is." - Valeri

Yet another woman writes:

"I was one of the many women who was tricked and deceived into believing I was David's wife. David came into my life in May of 2015. I was going through some things with my former husband (of 25 years) at the time. His assistant, reached out to me to view David Taylor teachings. I knew her previously before she became apart of J.M.M.I. I used to have weekly conference call with her. I was a mentor to her. Upon meeting a few times, like Vicki, he stated I was his wife but we must be secret about it, etc.

In December of 2016, I was asked to leave the ministry because I found out about the others. The threats increased as well as sending photos and videos of me, (which he begged for most of the time.) David E. Taylor is one of the biggest false Apostles, false Prophets, and womanizers of our day...May this book be the ultimate tool to destroy this false kingdom to open the eyes of the blind and set the captives free." -Septima

It is sad that so many women have lost so much because of one man. I wish I had my time back: countless months, weeks, days, and hours feeding his ego. He yearned for attention, praise, and gifts. I gave expensive gifts and money to both he and the ministry—only God can truly restore.

The (true) King David in scripture had a choice to make in the battle with the Philistine. He realized the battle was no longer personal. The battle was to fight on behalf of a people, a kingdom, and the armies of the Lord.

For who is this uncircumcised Philistine, that he should defy the armies of the living God?" And David said, "What have I done now? Is there not a cause?" Then he turned from him toward another and said the same thing; and these people answered him as the first ones did. —I Samuel 17:26-29

Indeed, I too ask the question,

"Is there not a cause?"

If you are consistently saying you are NOT in a cult like I did, YOU ARE IN A CULT!

USING YOUR VOICE

Your reflections from Chapter 7

_____

_____

_____

_____

_____

_____

_____

_____

_____

_____

_____

_____

TANYA WEST'S STORY

'M TANYA WEST. THIS is my real name. I too was a victim. Today, I'm free. I was one of the many women who was tricked and deceived into believing I was David Taylor's wife. David came into my life on October 17, 2017. I had no idea of the storm I was about to enter. It would become one of the darkest times and seasons of my life. David E. Taylor, I called my king. This is going to sound crazy I know, but I must tell it the way it happened. David would say, "A husband is a lord." Just like Sarah when she obeyed Abraham and acknowledged him as her authority headship. Sarah called Abraham lord. This is what Taylor desired of his "wife." And as his wife (married unto God) I was expected to be obedient in all things as the scriptures said of a wife. David E. Taylor wanted this type of submission. He would teach that a wife is to go after the desires of her husband's heart. Just like Esther wanted to please the king and do things the king's way.

David worked his way into my life by luring me into a false sense of trust. I was indoctrinated by his teachings of "The Mystery of Authority" and his "Kingdom of God" teachings and women's ministry teachings on rank. I was told that I had to willingly submit to him in love otherwise ranks and authority meant nothing. I was put in a position of feeling like I was going to fail my destiny if I didn't choose to be obedient in the moment of request. So, I was to obey him as my husband. I was also to obey his authority as an Apostle, and God's "face-to-face Prophet" in my life.

David started requesting naked pictures of me in different positions, in lingerie, and heels. He wanted these throughout the week as much as I could give him—at least one picture every day although not always nude. He then wanted me to do videos, at least two a week (more if I was willing,) by putting a demand on me to "obey and submit" to him as the scriptures say—thus I was being "obedient to God" in doing so. I begged for him to let me stop. I knew it was wrong. It was killing me deep down inside. I cried every day during this 17 month period. I lost almost 3/4 of my hair. I would say this to myself and to God, "Jesus doesn't save my life to kill my life." I felt isolated. I couldn't trust anyone about my situation. I was in something far bigger that I knew how to handle. After praying and genuinely seeking the Lord to get me out, He did. He got me out of the deception.

Satan studies our lives and strategically knows how to come at you with your desires. My desire was just to obey God's will. Satan could maximize on this knowing I want to be obedient to God. We know we are to obey God's Word. I knew before my involvement with Taylor that people have been twisting the word of God throughout history and it's no different today. I use to run from this type of manipulation and control. Yet, I was injected with the narcotics of the Narcissist unknowingly in the beginning which altered my mind under his influence. It shifted me off from the REAL truth. I was not myself, my real self. Those close enough to me and who knew me saw this. Never did I think this could happen to me. I started to think back to before Taylor came on the scene, what I knew God said. But Taylor was trying to convince me it was questionable, so I would doubt God's true Word.

I knew there was a purpose for what I had just walked through. God had a plan to use this for His glory for such a time as this. I had no idea God would use this dark season of my life and connect my destiny with Vicki's to help as a shining light to expose the abuse, dangers to women and others of this wicked deception that comes with David E. Taylor when you are aligned with him.

For such are false apostles, deceitful workers,transforming themselves into the apostles of Christ. And no marvel; for Satan himself is transformed into an angel of light. Therefore it is no great thing if his ministers also be transformed as the ministers of righteousness; whose end shall be according to their works. —*2 Corinthians 11:13-15*

David E. Taylor is a false Apostle and Prophet. May God's truth, justice, and mercy be upon all still involved and stuck in the deception of J.M.M.I. May this book open the eyes of the blind and set the captives free bringing healing and deliverance.

Speak up for those who cannot speak for themselves; ensure justice for those being crushed. Yes, speak up for the poor and helpless, and see that they get justice. —*Proverbs 31:8-9 NLT*

Vicki, it's because of your story of truth that I am free.

USING YOUR *Voice*

Your reflections from *Chapter* 8

_____

_____

_____

_____

_____

_____

_____

_____

_____

_____

_____

_____

---— $\mathscr{C}$HAPTER 9 ——---

ERICA ESKRIDGE'S STORY

'M ERICA ESKRIDGE. I was victimized and greatly deceived by David E. Taylor, a man who claims to be a man of God and Jesus' best friend. I first began to communicate with David via Facebook Messenger in the year of 2013. A friend of mine recommended I go to him to get a dream I had interpreted. I sent him a friend request. I was surprised how fast he accepted my request. Not only did he accept my request, but he messaged me saying, "Hello gorgeous you're so beautiful." My reaction was wow this great man of God is complimenting me. I responded, "Hi Man of God, I recently lost my father to lung cancer, and I need help interpreting my dream." David responded maybe 15 minutes after I messaged him, and that the Holy Spirit drew him to me.

He sent me pictures of me that he had found on my Facebook to Messenger saying, "I love this picture of you. You're so gorgeous." I said, "Thank you man of God." He went on asking me, "Where do you live? How many children do you have?" and so on. He told me he wanted to get to know me better. I told him I had just come out of a divorce. I wasn't ready to date. I needed to heal. David never stopped. He would always message me, "Hey beautiful. I love you so much. You're my wife." I immediately felt like he was an answer to prayer. I believed he was someone the Lord may have sent to be a blessing to me after experiencing so much heartache, disappointment, and loss. I thought the Lord was saying this would be a man that would love me genuinely for who I was. He would take good care of me. He would not misuse or manipulate me.

After almost a year of David trying to pursue me, I finally told him, yes we could date. In 2014, David invited me to a "One night with the King" on New Year's Eve. I went along with my family to finally meet David E. Taylor in person and to learn more about his ministry. Once we arrived to J.M.M.I., everything was so beautifully organized and had lots of food. I was impressed. I said to myself, "Wow, lucky me." Boy was I wrong. David had his staff escort me and my family to his office after the service. He met me and my family for the first time.

After my family left the office, David began to pace back and forth saying how beautiful I was. He said how much he loved me. He asked me if I ever went to Paris. I said, "No. I have never

"Why is a Man of God, kissing me inside a church?"

been to a different state." He seemed shocked saying, "Oh wow! I can't believe I'll be the first to take my baby on a plane." I told him I had to get going soon. David kissed me. I thought to myself, "Why is a Man of God kissing me inside a church?" I brushed it off—he's just a man. As I left the church, I got in the car with my family. David sent me a text telling me how excited he was when he saw me. I asked him if he could get a hotel room for my family because we were all tired. We didn't feel like getting on the road to drive five hours. David said, yes. He had his staff get us a room. I had no idea we would be booked at his hotel.

Once we were at the hotel, David texted me asking if I would come to his room. He gave me his room number. I went there. David had changed his clothes. I remember he asked me a few questions like my favorite color, so on. Later he began to kiss me and tried having sex with me. I told him no because it would mess things up. I wanted to wait to be married before sex.

David convinced me that it wasn't wrong because I was his wife and in God's timing, we would get married. He told me he was a man of the Spirit. He heard from God. If God tells him to marry me tomorrow, he would send for me and we would get married. We did not have sex.

Months later David sent for me to go to St. Louis. I was staying for two days. I noticed something strange however, once my flight arrived, his staff was there to pick me up. His staff dropped me off at a hotel telling me to get dressed that he would pick me up after I was ready. So, his staff came knocking on the door. I left the hotel. I grabbed all my belongings. The staff member told me I wasn't going back to the hotel. He drove me to David's mansion. David came downstairs dressed. They showed me around telling me what's his is mine. He showed me all the cars he had and told me I would drive the BMW drop-top. He showed me rooms. He said one room would be for my daughter (once we got married) and the boys rooms would be for my sons and his son. I was impressed after that.

David and I and went out for dinner. We came back to the house and went to his room. That night we had sex. Every time I would see him, we would have sex. I felt bad in the beginning because I knew it wasn't right in God's eyes. Somehow David made me feel so comfortable about who he was in my life, and that we would get married.

I believed his lies until one day Vicki Yohe reached out to me on Facebook Messenger exposing David.

I was in awe, so hurt, and confused. This man who I believed was Jesus' friend has been lying to me and many others all these years! I've invested so much believing he was my husband and someday we would get married. It was all a lie! I'm so thankful for Vicki Yohe. Thank you for sounding the alarm to set many free from this master manipulator David E. Taylor.

"Stand fast therefore in the liberty wherewith Christ hath made us free, and be not entangled again with the yoke of bondage." —Galatians 5:1

USING YOUR VOICE

Your reflections from Chapter 9

_____

_____

_____

_____

_____

_____

_____

_____

_____

_____

_____

_____

_____

_____

CHAPTER 10

DELORES COLES' STORY

I CAN PERSONALLY ATTEST to Vicki Yohe's allegations and the exposure of David E. Taylor. I hope the person reading this will be set free if they are entangled with him or J.M.M.I. You see, I was also ensnared with the self-proclaimed "LAST GREATEST END TIME GENERAL - APOSTLE DAVID E. TAYLOR". I was involved with this "Man of God" in an intimate relationship for nearly three years.

David came to me as a "Prophet" to "prophesy" a "word from God" for me. Oddly, in that same conversation, he told me God had showed him my heart and that I was HIS WIFE. He said I was a Prophetess, that he would "train me" in the prophetic gifts and take me under his wing. I said I was his queen who needs a king like him. He was an emperor and I was his empress, a lioness, all the things a woman loves to hear. At the time, I was considering marrying someone else. Neither was David my "type" nor was I interested in him. So, this was a challenge for him to woo me.

He quickly and heavily pursued me by sending flowers, CD's, books, gifts, chocolate covered strawberries, etc. I had no idea who he really was. So to build rapport, he would have his "staff" or "volunteers" may be the more appropriate word (since they work for free), vouch for his character. They would send me pictures from what appeared to be past crusades. Pictures of his cars, like his Bentley and Rolls Royce, and a private jet he claimed to have (but gave it all up for the church), to validate who he was. In turn, he would always ask for sexy/nude pictures, especially as the relationship progressed and we were communicating long distance.

Because he was a church leader, an Apostle, a "face-to-face" Prophet (he says), I believed the lie of being called to be his wife and believed he was a part of my "destiny." Within a short time, he would send for me. He would put me up in fancy hotels. I was invited to spend time with him whether he was preaching, or just to be with him and his family. (It all had to be kept in "SECRET") Yet, it was all under the pretense that I was his wife— and that when "God released the date," we would be married. Regretfully, I fell for his lies and manipulation tactics on how "God knows our hearts" so it's okay to have sex. He had a special immutable covenant with God, basically that he is above the "law".

It's all smoke and mirrors. Photos of past crusades, etc. were not from David filling up arenas. In fact, David is not endorsed or world renowned as he claims to be. His website bio says he has hundreds/ thousands of people and churches under his leadership. This is unfounded and only fills his ego and narcissist beliefs, not arenas—let alone a church with a capacity of any more than 100 people.

David twists the Word of God to fit his actions. He uses this to endorse his immoral lifestyle. He is a charlatan, a predator, preying on women via Facebook, scouring their nude pictures, asking for more pictures, as well as seducing the masses by preaching false humility. Get him behind closed doors and watch him make gay jokes and call his staff members "gay-blade", "pillow biters", etc. and then when he gets angry call them NEGRO - both the men and the women. It's appalling that any one ESPECIALLY IN LEADERSHIP would behave this way.

Once you start believing such GRANDEUR, it makes it hard to ever walk away because he operates in cult practices by instilling mind control of "forfeiting your destiny" and tries to CURSE you to sickness and death if you try to leave or speak out. David has a God Complex. He believes he is Jesus' BEST FRIEND and that he sits next to God the Father with Jesus. He submits to no one. No one of any weight or good reputation in ministry supports this nonsense. He has no accountability whatsoever for his actions public or private in "molesting" me and countless others spiritually.

I have repented of any involvement with this false Prophet and am guilty of ignoring my gut instincts. I had received many warnings from both men and women on Facebook that he was a whoremonger and promised to marry many women. It wasn't until I got into his Facebook account as he slept that I discovered the multitudes of women of every race, size, and age. Some were single, married, divorced who he was pursuing in the same manner and telling us ALL the same thing.

I pray for those sowing into his "ministry"

by way of cash, jewelry, money, cars, etc. David is manipulating everyone, especially women all across the world—using their "seed money" to fly women in and out of whatever city he is in. He puts himself and the women up in the finest hotels, wining and dining them. David E. Taylor is an opportunist. He is nothing short of a master manipulator, "prophelying" crook swindling people and using GOD'S MONEY to fund his lifestyle.

I also pray for everyone reading this to open their eyes and get delivered, set FREE from the cult leadership of David E. Taylor and J.M.M.I. Don't believe the lies or the curses he tries to put on you and your family. God sees. He loves you so much. He does not want to see you caught up in this wickedness when He brings judgment. You are too precious to Him.

"No weapon that is formed against thee shall prosper; and every tongue that shall rise against thee in judgment thou shalt condemn. This is the heritage of the servants of the Lord, and their righteousness is of me, saith the Lord."

—Isaiah 54:17

USING YOUR VOICE

Your reflections from Chapter 10

_____

_____

_____

_____

_____

_____

_____

_____

_____

_____

_____

CHAPTER 11

FACTS THAT WILL SAVE YOUR LIFE

KEEP YOUR EYES ON Jesus (Stay focused on what matters most.)

- Stay in the Word (If it contradicts basic scripture, GET OUT!)

- Never keep a secret relationship (If it can't be made public or exposed to the light, run)

- Never tolerate any type of abuse (Including: Physical, Emotional, Mental, Financial, Spiritual, or Verbal)

- Do your research (Get all the information. Talk to

the right people. Check out their history and who or what they are connected to. Guard Your Heart!)

- Listen to the voice of God (He screamed and yelled at someone one time about furniture. He belittled him, called him a stupid idiot. I cried, and felt very bad for him. I believe I heard the voice of God saying "get your boys and get out of here." I didn't listen.)

Please pay attention and use these facts, they will save your life!

My son, forget not my law; but let thine heart keep my commandments: For length of days, and long life, and peace, shall they add to thee. Let not mercy and truth forsake thee: bind them about thy neck; write them upon the table of thine heart: So shalt thou find favour and good understanding in the sight of God and man. Trust in the Lord with all thine heart; and lean not unto thine own understanding. In all thy ways acknowledge him, and he shall direct thy paths.

Be not wise in thine own eyes: fear the Lord, and depart from evil. It shall be health to thy navel, and marrow to thy bones. Honour the Lord with thy substance, and with the firstfruits of all thine increase: So shall thy barns be filled with plenty, and thy presses shall burst out with new wine. My son, despise not the chastening of the Lord; neither be weary of his correction: For whom the

Lord loveth he correcteth; even as a father the son in whom he delighteth Happy is the man that findeth wisdom, and the man that getteth understanding. For the merchandise of it is better than the merchandise of silver, and the gain thereof than fine gold. She is more precious than rubies: and all the things thou canst desire are not to be compared unto her length of days is in her right hand; and in her left hand riches and honour. Her ways are ways of pleasantness, and all her paths are peace. She is a tree of life to them that lay hold upon her: and happy is every one that retaineth her.

The Lord by wisdom hath founded the earth; by understanding hath he established the heavens. By his knowledge the depths are broken up, and the clouds drop down the dew. My son, let not them depart from thine eyes: keep sound wisdom and discretion: So shall they be life unto thy soul, and grace to thy neck. Then shalt thou walk in thy way safely, and thy foot shall not stumble. When thou liest down, thou shalt not be afraid: yea, thou shalt lie down, and thy sleep shall be sweet.

Be not afraid of sudden fear, neither of the desolation of the wicked, when it cometh. For the Lord shall be thy confidence, and shall keep thy foot from being taken. Withhold not good from them to whom it is due, when it is in the power of thine hand to do it. Say not unto thy neighbour, Go, and come again, and to morrow I will give;

when thou hast it by thee. Devise not evil against thy neighbour, seeing he dwelleth securely by thee.

Strive not with a man without cause, if he have done thee no harm. Envy thou not the oppressor, and choose none of his ways. For the froward is abomination to the Lord: but his secret is with the righteous. The curse of the Lord is in the house of the wicked: but he blesseth the habitation of the just. Surely he scorneth the scorners: but he giveth grace unto the lowly. The wise shall inherit glory: but shame shall be the promotion of fools.
—Proverbs 3

USING YOUR VOICE

Your reflections from Chapter 11

_____

_____

_____

_____

_____

_____

_____

_____

_____

_____

_____

_____

CHAPTER 12

"BECAUSE OF WHO YOU ARE" PROFILE OF A CULT LEADER

I T IS VITAL THAT you understand the very profile of a cult leader. Careful and prayerful research will reveal so much. A former FBI agent had this to say:

"One of the questions that I am often asked by students of criminology and psychology is, how do you know when a cult leader is "evil" or "bad"? These of course are vague descriptors to some extent, but I also get the question, "When is a cult leader pathological or a danger to others?" This is a valid question in view of the historical record

of suffering and hurt caused by various cult leaders around the world.

From my studies of cults and cult leaders during my time in the FBI, I learned early on that there are some things to look for that, at a minimum, say "caution, this individual is dangerous, and in all likelihood will cause harm to others."

Having studied at length the life, teachings, and behaviors of Jim Jones (Jonestown Guyana), David Koresh (Branch Davidians), Stewart Traill (The Church of Bible Understanding), Charles Manson, Shoko Asahara (Aum Shinrikyo), Joseph Di Mambro (The Order of the Solar Temple a.k.a. Ordre du Temple Solaire), Marshall Heff Applewhit (Heaven's Gate), Bhagwan Rajneesh (Rajneesh Movement), and Warren Jeffs (polygamist leader), I can say that what stands out about these individuals is that they were or are all pathologically narcissistic. They all have or had an over-abundant belief that they were special, that they and they alone had the answers to problems, and that they had to be revered. They demanded perfect loyalty from followers, they overvalued themselves and devalued those around them, they were intolerant of criticism, and above all they did not like being questioned or challenged. And yet, in spite of these less than charming traits, they had no trouble attracting those who were willing to overlook these features.

These personality traits stand out as the first warning to those who would associate with them, but there are many others. Here is a collection of traits of cult leaders that give us hints as to their psychopathology. This list is not all-inclusive nor is it the final word on the subject; it is merely my personal collection based on studies and interviews that I conducted in my previous career.

If you know of a cult leader who has many of these traits there is a high probability that they are hurting those around them emotionally, psychologically, physically, spiritually, or financially. And of course this does not take into account the hurt that their loved ones will also experience.

Here are the typical traits of the pathological cult leader (from Dangerous Personalities) that you should watch for:

1. He has a grandiose idea of who he is and what he can achieve.

2. Is preoccupied with fantasies of unlimited success, power, or brilliance.

3. *Demands blind, unquestioned obedience.*

4. *Requires excessive admiration from followers and outsiders.*

5. *Has a sense of entitlement—expecting to be treated as special at all times.*

6. *Is exploitative of others by asking for their money or that of relatives, putting others at financial risk.*

7. *Is arrogant and haughty in his behavior or attitude.*

8. *Has an exaggerated sense of power (entitlement) that allows him to bend rules and break laws.*

9. *Takes sexual advantage of members of his sect or cult.*

10. *Sex is a requirement with adults and sub adults as part of a ritual or rite.*

11. *Is hypersensitive to how he is seen or perceived by others.*

12. *Publicly devalues others as being inferior, incapable, or not worthy.*

13. *Makes members confess their sins or faults, publicly subjecting them to ridicule or humiliation while revealing exploitable*

weaknesses of the penitent.

14.   *Has ignored the needs of others, including: biological, physical, emotional, and financial needs.*

15.   *Is frequently boastful of accomplishments.*

16.   *Needs to be the center of attention and does things to distract others to ensure that he or she is being noticed, e.g., by arriving late, using exotic clothing, overdramatic speech, or by making theatrical entrances.*

17.   *Has insisted on always having the best of anything (house, car, jewelry, clothes) even when others are relegated to lesser facilities, amenities, or clothing.*

18.   *Doesn't seem to listen well to needs of others; communication is usually one-way, in the form of dictates.*

19.   *Haughtiness, grandiosity, and the need to be controlling is part of his personality.*

20.   *Behaves as though people are objects to be used, manipulated or exploited for personal gain.*

21.   *When criticized he tends to lash out not just with anger but with rage.*

22.   *Anyone who criticizes or questions him is called an "enemy."*

23.   *Refers to non-members or non-believers*

as "the enemy."

24. *Acts imperious at times, not wishing to know what others think or desire.*

25. *Believes himself to be omnipotent.*

26. *Has "magical" answers or solutions to problems.*

27. *Is superficially charming.*

28. *Habitually puts down others as inferior; only he is superior.*

29. *Has a certain coldness or aloofness about him that makes others worry about who this person really is and or whether they really know him.*

30. *Is deeply offended when there are perceived signs of boredom, being ignored or of being slighted.*

31. *Treats others with contempt and arrogance.*

32. *Is constantly assessing people to determine those who are a threat or those who revere him.*

33. *The word "I" dominates his conversations. He is oblivious to how often he references himself.*

34. *Hates to be embarrassed or fail publicly; when he does he acts out with rage.*

35.   Doesn't seem to feel guilty for anything he has done wrong nor does he apologize for his actions.

36.   Believes he possesses the answers and solutions to world problems.

37.   Believes himself to be a deity or a chosen representative of a deity.

38.   "Rigid," "unbending," or "insensitive" describes how this person thinks.

39.   Tries to control others in what they do, read, view, or think.

40.   Has isolated members of his sect from contact with family or the outside world.

41.   Monitors and/or restricts contact with family or outsiders.

42.   Works the least but demands the most.

43.   Has stated that he is "destined for greatness" or that he will be "martyred."

44.   Seems to be highly dependent on tribute and adoration and will often fish for compliments.

45.   Uses enforcers or sycophants to ensure compliance from members or believers.

46.   Sees self as "unstoppable" and perhaps has even said so.

47.   Conceals background or family, which

would disclose how plain or ordinary he is.

48.   *Doesn't think there is anything wrong with himself and in fact sees himself as perfection or "blessed."*

49.   *Has taken away followers' freedom to leave, to travel, to pursue life and liberty.*

50.   *Has isolated the group physically (moved to a remote area) so as to not be observed.*

When the question is asked, "When do we know when a cult leader is bad, or evil, or toxic?" this is the list that I use to survey the cult leader for dangerous traits. Of course the only way to know anything for sure is to observe and validate, but these characteristics can go a long way to help with that. And as I have said, there are other things to look for and there may be other lists, but this is the one that I found most useful from studying these groups and talking to former members of cults.

When a cult or organizational leader has a preponderance of these traits then we can anticipate that at some point those who associate with him will likely suffer physically, emotionally, psychologically, or financially. If these traits sound familiar to leaders, groups, sects, or organizations known to you, then expect those who associate with them to live in despair and to suffer, even if they don't know yet that they will." - Joe Navarro[11], former FBI Counterintelligence Agent

The Branch Davidian cult made national headlines on February 28, 1993, when its Waco Texas property was seized by Federal Agents. After a very long standoff, 80 people, agents, and the Cult's leader, "David Koresh" were killed. David, whose real name was Vernon Howell, manipulated his way to the "Prophet" and spiritual authority of the group. He changed his name to David to suggest that he was a spiritual heir of the biblical King, David. "Koresh" which is Hebrew for Cyrus was the ancient Persian King.

Koresh quickly abused his new "authority" by taking several "spiritual" wives from the group. If you were married and he wanted your wife, he would simply break up the marriage. In fact, no one was allowed to be in covenant except him. He claimed the women belong to him and they were of the "House of David." He had financial problems and scams as well. David Koresh felt he was the last/final end time Prophet preparing the world for what was to come. He even challenged another leader in the group into a "dual of power." He told the man to prove his power, and David would prove that his was greater. When a former member was asked how and why they were involved in such deception. They said,

"I'll call it a cult, that's what it was ... it's people doing things they wouldn't normally do, like giving up their wives and letting their children have sex with adults, which is crazy, but that's what you do when you're in a cult. You are under someone else's control," former member Mr. Bunds once said to ABC News. "His message also changed over and over because he was always looking for the next big thing to teach that would shock people into listening to him."

David would always mention the constant persecution he was under by the many "haters" he claim to have. He once told me,

"It's because they don't believe anyone can see Jesus."

Similarly, his followers have said he has "given up so much—sacrificed so much." The "persecution," as he calls it, has nothing to do with "face-to-face," or seeing Jesus. It has everything to do with what I'm exposing in this book.

EXPOSURE IS NOT PERSECUTION!

Vicki Yohe's Creed for All Women

I speak for all women of all ages, enough is enough!

We will NOT be silenced!

We will not believe the lies you tell us!

We will keep no secrets!

We are Valuable. We are Beautiful. We are Daughters of the King!

We speak our truth with boldness!

Your threats won't shut us up!

Beware; we are Women of God who know who we are!

We are Victorious!

"It feels great being on the side of righteousness and having the Favor of God."

USING YOUR VOICE

Your reflections from Chapter 12

_____

_____

_____

_____

_____

_____

_____

_____

_____

_____

_____

_____

_____

_____

—— CHAPTER 13 ——

TRAITS OF TOXIC MEN

Signs of Toxic and Manipulative Men
By Family Therapist, Jolie Warren[12] (edited)

1. Gaslighting and crazy-making.

Gaslighting typically happens very gradually in a relationship; in fact, his actions may seem harmless at first. Over time, however, abusive patterns continue and you can become confused, anxious, isolated, and depressed, and can lose all sense of what is actually happening. Then you'll start relying on the abusive man more and more to define your reality, which creates a very difficult situation to escape.

If he says and does things that cause confusion or you to feel like you are crazy, you're being gaslighted. If you're being gaslighted you'll feel self-doubt, question whether or not you are being overly emotional, become insecure in your role in the relationship and find yourself apologizing for everything that goes wrong in the relationship. It's psychologically dangerous, get out!

2. Unable to see things from your perspective.

He says something or does something that causes you emotional pain. You attempt to explain to him how you feel but are met with a blank stare or annoyance. He isn't someone who can see things from your perspective. He isn't someone who can understand why his actions had any impact on you, negative or positive.

He is the kind of guy who says to you, "I'm not responsible for your feelings." If he cheats on you, he wants you to get over it. If he doesn't show up for a planned date, he accuses you of being uptight and controlling. He is a jerk!

3. The ultimate hypocrite.

"Do as I say, not as I do." He has

extremely high expectations for fidelity, respect, and adoration. After the idealization phase, he will give none of this back to you. He will cheat, lie, criticize, and manipulate. But you are expected to remain perfect, otherwise, you will promptly be replaced and deemed unstable.

4. Pathological lying.

Before you even question him about a subject or situation he'll have a lie ready to tell you. And, when caught lying, he expresses no remorse or embarrassment. He just tries to lie his way out of the original lie. His life is one big lie and so are his feelings for you.

5. He focuses on your mistakes but ignores his own.

This guy needs you to be perfect and to view him as perfect in spite of his bad behavior. Your mistakes will be brought to your attention. He will expect you to be remorseful and to make changes as he sees fit. He, on the other hand, can do no wrong and you better not forget that.

6. The meaning of respect is lost on him.

Normal people understand fundamental concepts like honesty and kindness. The toxic man is childlike in his ability to grasp the concept of not only receiving respect but returning it.

He won't respect your need for time alone or time with family and friends. He doesn't respect your boundaries, your career or, your desire to go to the bathroom without an audience. You can tell him dinner is promptly at 8:00 and he will show at 9:00. This guy is downright unmannerly, course and contemptible. Get as far away as possible!

7. Needs to be the center of attention.

This guy wants all your attention, 24/7 your life is supposed to revolve around him. His demand for adoration from you is insatiable. In reality, this guy has no identity without you there to constantly build him up. And, it isn't even about you. Anyone can give him what he needs…attention. You're only there because you were the first or fifth he found to do his bidding.

8. Assigns false emotions to you.

He will dismiss your true feelings and assign you feelings that most often mimic what he is feeling. Psychologist and psychiatrists called this "projection." Projection is a psychological defense mechanism in which he attributes characteristics he finds unacceptable in himself to another person…you.

For example, he may accuse you of wanting to have an affair or being attracted to a close friend or ex. In reality, it is him who may be having an affair or thinking about an affair or, attracted to someone other than you. He has projected his feelings of shame, guilt or desire for someone else off onto you because subconsciously he knows it's wrong but can't emotionally face that in himself.

9. Your gut is constantly telling you to investigate.

He has been caught in enough lies that you've finally gotten to the point of believing nothing he says. But you've also learned to doubt your own gut feelings so, you turn yourself into a private investigator and start stalking him on social media.

Or, maybe following him after work or driving by his home when you two aren't together. You're seeking answers to questions and doubts you have that you just can quite explain.

10. Everyone around you thinks he walks on water.

Everyone but you! But there must be something wrong with you if you're the only one questioning his values, morals, and sincerity. Here is what you need to keep in mind. You're the only one engaged in an intimate relationship with him. No one sees the side of him you see.

His relationship with those other people is superficial and that is why they don't see what you see in him!

11. You begin to fear expressing your feelings.

Normal couples argue to resolve issues, but toxic men make it clear that negative conversations will jeopardize the relationship, especially conversations regarding their bad behavior. Any of your attempts to improve communication will typically result in the silent treatment. You apologize and forgive quickly, otherwise, you know he'll lose interest in you.

12. He disrespects your boundaries.

Boundaries are guidelines, rules or limits that a person creates to identify for herself what are reasonable, safe and permissible ways for other people to behave around her and how she will respond when someone steps outside those limits.

If he is repeatedly crossing your boundaries, he isn't willing to discuss boundaries with you, or you notice he is guilt-tripping you for even having boundaries, your relationship is likely very unhealthy and could become abusive if his behaviors continue and escalate.

13. They belittle and dismiss you.

If you point this out, they call you sensitive and crazy. You might begin to feel resentful and upset, but you learn to push away those feelings in favor of maintaining the peace. They withhold attention and undermine your self-esteem. After once showering you with nonstop attention and admiration, they suddenly seem completely bored by you.

They treat you with silence and become very annoyed that you're interested in continuing the passionate relationship they created with you. You begin to feel like a chore to them.

14. You're supposed to be a mind reader.

He doesn't communicate his needs or plans with you. If he gets exasperated because you fail to do something he wanted but you didn't know about, you're on the hook because you failed to read his mind.

Guys like this are non-communicators. They are immature romantics who believe, "if she really loved me, she'd know what I need." You can't win with this guy because they like to play the victim and what better way to do that than leave you to wonder what they want and need from you.

15. You feel anxious but can't define why.

Bad relationships will eventually cause anxiety. If you find yourself suddenly feeling unexplained anxiety take a long, hard look at the dynamics of your relationship with him.

If you're in a relationship with a toxic man you're most likely constantly stressed out over the state of the relationship, or over-analyzing the constant conflict in the relationship. You probably don't need meds for anxiety just a new relationship partner!

16. He has a dysfunctional past.

Some toxic men have serious mental health problems and they always have someone to blame them on. If all his exes were witches, his parents were neglectful and his childhood friends and work friends are all defective... according to him, you can bet his dysfunctional past isn't about all those people and all about him.

This guy is so messed up that you can bet he will mess up any relationship he engages in, romantic and otherwise.

17. Stirs the pot, loves conflict.

He is a drama queen! He is always putting his nose into other peoples' business and conflicts. He isn't happy and doesn't want anyone else to be either. He will not be able to get along with your girlfriends. He won't have friends of his own because he ran them off with his meddling.

This guy is addicted to the adrenaline rush he gets from engaging in conflict. If there isn't conflict going on, he will find a way to start it.

18. He is in LOVE!

When you first meet, things move extremely fast. He tells you how much he has in common with you—how perfect you are for him. After the first date, he has changed his Facebook status to, "in a relationship."

He constantly initiates communication and seems to be fascinated with you on every level. You met him on July 3rd and he is already planning a Christmas getaway for the two of you after only two weeks. He is all about pinning you down quickly.

By Christmas there will be no trip, he will have lost interest and you'll be licking your emotional wounds because you fell for his game, hook, line and sinker.

19. Compares you to other people.

They compare you to ex-lovers, friends, family members, and your eventual replacement. When idealizing, they make you feel special by telling you how much better you are than these people. When devaluing, they use these comparisons to make you feel jealous and inferior.

20. Your admirable qualities become deficiencies.

At first, they appeal to your deepest vanities and vulnerabilities, observing and mimicking exactly what they think you want to hear. But after you're hooked, they start to use these things against you. You spend more and more time trying to prove yourself worthy to the very same person who once said you were perfect.

USING YOUR VOICE

Your reflections from Chapter 13

_____

_____

_____

_____

_____

_____

_____

_____

_____

_____

CHAPTER 14

LIVING WATERS

MANY TIMES IN THE church, when someone falls, or makes a mistake they are not only talked about, but they are treated like lepers. No one wants anything to do with you. You are left alone. You feel ashamed and sorrowful that you let people down who looked up to you—those that feel like you should be above this. Regardless of your supporters, your family and friends, you need to be able to look yourself in the mirror. You need to be able to sleep at night knowing you have come clean, you were transparent, and you were honest and open. This is a place of considerable vulnerability. It is also a place of true victory. I exposed myself. It freed me.

As He spake these words, many believed on Him. Then said Jesus to those Jews which believed on Him, If ye continue in My word, then are ye My disciples indeed; And ye shall know the truth, and the truth shall make you free. They answered Him, we be Abraham's seed, and were never in bondage to any man: how sayest thou, Ye shall be made free? Jesus answered them, Verily, verily, I say unto you, Whosoever committeth sin is the servant of sin. And the servant abideth not in the house for ever: but the Son abideth ever. If the Son therefore shall make you free, ye shall be free indeed.
—John 8:30-36

When true people of God had provided an opportunity for me to receive counseling ministry, I had no idea how much healing would take place. I had never gone through counseling or anything like that. When I arrived at the facility, I couldn't see tomorrow. I was so depressed. Over the week that I was there, God ministered healing and restoration to me. One thing I said during an interview was, "God specializes in mending broken hearts." God used Pastor Denise Boggs of Living Waters to go deep and help me discover what was broken in me. Abuse from childhood, the secrets—things from ministry and things you just don't ever share or talk about much. God gave me a heart transplant. This is what He does. He removes the stone in our hearts and makes it anew. He gives us that living water to make us whole again and again.

"This is what He does. He removes the stone in our hearts and makes it anew."

Then cometh He to a city of Samaria, which is called Sychar, near to the parcel of ground that Jacob gave to his son Joseph. Now Jacob's well was there. Jesus therefore, being wearied with his journey, sat thus on the well: and it was about the sixth hour. There cometh a woman of Samaria to draw water: Jesus saith unto her, Give Me to drink.(For his disciples were gone away unto the city to buy meat.) Then saith the woman of Samaria unto Him, How is it that thou, being a Jew, askest drink of me, which am a woman of Samaria? for the Jews have no dealings with the Samaritans. Jesus answered and said unto her, If thou knewest the gift of God, and Who it is that saith to thee, Give Me to drink; thou wouldest have asked of Him, and He would have given thee living water. The woman saith unto Him, Sir, thou hast nothing to draw with, and the well is deep: from whence then hast thou that living water? Art thou greater than our father Jacob, which gave us the well, and drank thereof himself, and his children, and his cattle? Jesus answered and said unto her, Whosoever drinketh of this water shall thirst again: But whosoever drinketh of the water that I shall give him shall never thirst; but the water that I shall give him shall be in him a well of water springing up into everlasting life. The woman saith unto Him, Sir, give me this water, that I thirst not, neither come hither to draw. —John 4:5-15

When it was time to leave,

I was sad. I didn't want to leave.

I had found my "safe place."

There was much ministry to my soul and spirit.

I loved the worship.

Worship music would play during the night.

I would wake every morning surrounded by the peace of God.

God did a true work in me.

I felt like I had hope.

I was truly excited about my future again. What an awesome God we serve!

During my process of restoration, I sat myself down from ministry for a year. Yes, this hurt me financially, but healed me spiritually. I had repented, and was on my road to restoration and recovery.

My future is amazing in Jesus' Name! I have a new assignment and ministry helping women. I believe I'm an "Esther" to a people who have been through what I have been through and am going through; God is still doing a work. My two boys mean the world to me. I will be a better Mom, help develop them for their future and destiny in life and in the things of God. It is my desire to teach and continue writing books. God wants me to use my voice not only in singing, but in so many other ways.

For I know the thoughts that I think toward you, saith the Lord, thoughts of peace, and not of evil, to give you an expected end. —Jeremiah 29:11

I said to David, "I thought you loved me."

He replied, "You believed the lie."

David E. Taylor will not have the last word in this book, God will. He told his followers one time, "I dress nice, but I live low." Most haven't seen the cars and his lavish lifestyle. They believe his false humility. His staff knows the truth.

After I went public and confessed my sin, David and three of his staff members still tried hard to discredit me with all sorts of stories and lies. Anyone who knows me or has been connected to my ministry (over the last three decades,) knows theses things are ridiculous.

David claims he had been "counseling" me for a drug addiction. Further, I was removed from J.M.M.I. for not receiving his counsel. All of these are lies and are laughable attempts to deny our relationship. David denies all of his relationships when confronted. However, he can't manipulate God.

But the fearful, and unbelieving, and the abominable, and murderers, and whoremongers, and sorcerers, and idolaters, and all liars, shall have their part in the lake which burneth with fire and brimstone: which is the second death.
—Revelation 21:8

I'M AT PEACE

Even though my heart is breaking
I'm at peace
I never thought I would be shaken
But You came and laid Your hands on me and now
Oh oh Lord, You came and laid Your hands on me and now
I can see, my storm has moved away
I'm at peace
Even though I'm not worthy
I'm at peace
Even though I cannot see
Oh oh Lord, You died for me on Calvary and now
Oh oh, You died for me on Calvary and now
I can see, my storm
My storm has moved away

You came and laid Your hands on me and now
I can see clearly now the rain is gone
You came and laid Your hands on me and now
It will be all over in the morning
You came and laid Your hand on me and now
I can see, my storm has moved away

USING YOUR *Voice*

Your reflections from *Chapter* 14

_____

_____

_____

_____

_____

_____

_____

_____

_____

_____

_____

_____

WORD/PRAYER

As you progress through this month and end this year I pray for supernatural strength, health, increase, progress and success!

This day I nullify and prohibit from manifesting every satanic plot to sabotage the move of God in your life within the next and final days of this year. Let setbacks, sieges, delays, interruptions and interference cease and desist immediately and without delay! You are seated in heavenly places, and it is from this realm I decree and come into agreement with the total alignment of every area of your life that may be misaligned to purpose! I decree victorious and favorable outcomes in every battle you face! I legalize, quicken, call to life, establish and legislate supernatural blessings, an open heaven and favour, by the executive orders from Heaven, through the blood and Lordship of Jesus Christ! Right now in Jesus' name, no weapons of distraction, destruction, discouragement, frustrations or hindrance formed against you shall prosper! No attack on your mind or body shall prosper! By His stripes you are healed! You will no longer be disappointed nor disgraced by anyone or any situation! I pray supernatural strength, grace, wisdom, insight and divine empowerment upon you and further declare that you will finish this year strong! May every area of your life blossom!

May your plans and personal projects succeed! May God exceed your expectations! May your health be optimized! May your body, soul and spirit be rejuvenated! May the heavens be opened throughout the remaining of your life span! May your brand grow stronger and stronger in the market place! May the equity in your name increase in brand distinction, appeal and recognition! May God continue to increase your global influence! May your strategies be effective! May your dreams and goals become a reality! May your loved ones prosper! May all irritations and antagonisms cease! May your home be a haven of peace! Whatever you do shall prosper! I call you blessed, strong, loved, successful, focused and cherished! In Jesus' mighty name. God's promise to you:

Isaiah 65:21-23

"And they shall build houses, and inhabit them;and they shall plant vineyards, and eat the fruit of them. They shall not build, and another inhabit; they shall not plant,and another eat: for as the days of a tree are the days of my people, and mine elect shall long enjoy the work of their hands. They shall not labour in vain, nor bring forth for trouble; for they are the seed of the blessed of the Lord, and their offspring with them."

Go forth! Prevail! Succeed! Prosper!

Receive the blessings of Deut. 1:11 and Psalms 126:1-3 as benediction! Much love always!

Dr. Cindy Trimm

RESOURCES

1. The National Association of Christian Recovery

https://www.nacr.org/abusecenter/spiritual-abuse

2. The Learning Mind

https://www.learning-mind.com/spiritual-abuse-cults/

3. Spiritual Abuse Christian Cults and controlling Ministries

https://www.charismanews.com/opinion/32305-spiritual-abuse-christian-cults-and-controlling-ministries

4. Apologetics index (Spiritual Abuse)

http://www.apologeticsindex.org/8006-spiritual-abuse

5. The National Domestic Violence Hotline

https://www.thehotline.org/2015/11/12/what-is-spiritual-abuse

6. Information And Articles on Cults, Abuse, Grace And Legalism

www.spiritualabuse.org/articles.html

7. Spiritual Abuse and Cult Awareness
https://dallascult.com/

8. Spiritual Abuse and Cult Recovery - The Therapist's Bookshelf

https://thetherapistsbookshelf.com/clinical-issues/trauma/spiritual-abuse

Living Waters Ministry

Pastors Lee and Denise Boggs, Co-Founders

HEALING
HEARTS.
RESTORING
FAMILIES.

"But whoever drinks the water I give them
will never thirst." John 4:14

The vision of Living Waters Ministry is to create a safe place
where individuals, pastors, and couples can work through the
pain of their past, current problems, and burn-out situations, to
begin on a path of healing.

www.livingwatersministry.com

Address: 4803 Old Vashti Rd. • Hiddenite, NC 28636

Phone: 828-632-3906

SCRIPTURES TO ENCOURAGE

Encouraging Bible Verses about Strength

Philippians 4:13

I can do all things through Him who strengthens me.

Isaiah 41:10

Fear not, for I am with you; be not dismayed, for I am your God; I will strengthen you, I will help you, I will uphold you with my righteous right hand.

Deuteronomy 31:6

Be strong and courageous. Do not fear or be in dread of them, for it is the Lord your God who goes with you. He will not leave you or forsake you.

Isaiah 40:31

But they who wait for the Lord shall renew their strength; they shall mount up with wings like eagles; they shall run and not be weary; they shall walk and not faint.

1 Corinthians 10:13

No temptation has overtaken you that is not common to man. God is faithful, and he will not let you be tempted beyond your ability, but with the temptation he will also provide the way of escape, that you may be able to endure it.

Exodus 15:2

The Lord is my strength and my song, and he has become my salvation; this is my God, and I will praise Him, my father's God, and I will exalt Him.

Ephesians 6:10

Finally, be strong in the Lord and in the strength of His might.

Deuteronomy 20:4

For the Lord your God is he who goes with you to fight for you against your enemies, to give you the victory.

2 Corinthians 12:9-10

But he said to me, "My grace is sufficient for you, for my power is made perfect in weakness." Therefore I will boast all the more gladly of my weaknesses, so that the power of Christ may rest upon me. For the sake of Christ, then, I am content with weaknesses, insults, hardships, persecutions, and calamities. For when I am weak, then I am strong.

Joshua 1:9

Have I not commanded you? Be strong and courageous. Do not be frightened, and do not be dismayed, for the Lord your God is with you wherever you go.

2 Timothy 1:7

For God gave us a spirit not of fear but of power and love and self-control.

Isaiah 12:2

"Behold, God is my salvation; I will trust, and will not be afraid; for the Lord God is my strength and my song, and he has become my salvation."

Matthew 11:28

Come to me, all who labor and are heavy laden, and I will give you rest.

Isaiah 40:29

He gives power to the faint, and to him who has no might he increases strength.

Psalm 27:1

Of David. The Lord is my light and my salvation; whom shall I fear? The Lord is the stronghold of my life; of whom shall I be afraid?

Psalm 31:24

Be strong, and let your heart take courage, all you who wait for the Lord!

Psalm 73:26

My flesh and my heart may fail, but God is the strength of my heart and my portion forever.

2 Corinthians 12:9

But he said to me, "My grace is sufficient for you, for my power is made perfect in weakness." Therefore I will boast all the more gladly of my weaknesses, so that the power of Christ may rest upon me.

Mark 12:30

And you shall love the Lord your God with all your heart and with all your soul and with all your mind and with all your strength.'

Nehemiah 8:10

Then he said to them, "Go your way. Eat the fat and drink sweet wine and send portions to anyone who has nothing ready, for this day is holy to our Lord. And do not be grieved, for the joy of the Lord is your strength."

Psalm 46:1

To the choirmaster. Of the Sons of Korah. According to Alamoth. A Song. God is our refuge and strength, a very present help in trouble.

Habakkuk 3:19

God, the Lord, is my strength; he makes my feet like the deer's; he makes me tread on my high places. To the choirmaster: with stringed instruments.

Psalm 29:11

May the Lord give strength to His people! May the Lord bless His people with peace!

John 16:33

I have said these things to you, that in me you may have peace. In the world you will have tribulation. But take heart; I have overcome the world."

1 Peter 4:11

Whoever speaks, as one who speaks oracles of God; whoever serves, as one who serves by the strength that God supplies—in order that in everything God may be glorified through Jesus Christ. To him belong glory and dominion forever and ever. Amen.

Matthew 6:33

But seek first the kingdom of God and His righteousness, and all these things will be added to you.

Psalm 23:4

Even though I walk through the valley of the shadow of death, I will fear no evil, for you are with me; your rod and your staff, they comfort me.

2 Timothy 4:17

But the Lord stood by me and strengthened me, so that through me the message might be fully proclaimed and all the Gentiles might hear it. So I was rescued from the lion's mouth.

Psalm 118:14

The Lord is my strength and my song; he has become my salvation.

2 Thessalonians 3:3

But the Lord is faithful. He will establish you and guard you against the evil one.

Comforting Bible Verses about Love

1 Corinthians 13:4-8

Love is patient and kind; love does not envy or
boast; it is not arrogant or rude. It does not insist on
its own way; it is not irritable or resentful; it does not
rejoice at wrongdoing, but rejoices with the truth.
Love bears all things, believes all things, hopes all
things, endures all things. Love never ends. As for
prophecies, they will pass away; as for tongues,
they will cease; as for knowledge, it will pass away.

1 Corinthians 16:14

Let all that you do be done in love.

1 John 4:8

Anyone who does not love does not know God,
because God is love.

John 3:16

"For God so loved the world, that he gave His only
Son, that whoever believes in Him should not perish
but have eternal life.

John 13:34-35

A new commandment I give to you, that you love

one another: just as I have loved you, you also are to love one another. By this all people will know that you are my disciples, if you have love for one another.

Colossians 3:14

And above all these put on love, which binds everything together in perfect harmony.

1 Peter 4:8

Above all, keep loving one another earnestly, since love covers a multitude of sins.

John 15:13

Greater love has no one than this, that someone lay down His life for His friends.

Mark 12:29-31

Jesus answered, "The most important is, 'Hear, O Israel: The Lord our God, the Lord is one. And you shall love the Lord your God with all your heart and with all your soul and with all your mind and with all your strength.' The second is this: 'You shall love your neighbor as yourself.' There is no other commandment greater than these."

1 Corinthians 13:13

So now faith, hope, and love abide, these three; but the greatest of these is love.

Romans 5:8

But God shows His love for us in that while we were still sinners, Christ died for us.

Ephesians 4:2

With all humility and gentleness, with patience, bearing with one another in love,

Proverbs 17:17

A friend loves at all times, and a brother is born for adversity.

Romans 12:9

Let love be genuine. Abhor what is evil; hold fast to what is good.

1 John 4:16

So we have come to know and to believe the love that God has for us. God is love, and whoever abides in love abides in God, and God abides in Him.

Luke 6:35

But love your enemies, and do good, and lend,

expecting nothing in return, and your reward will be great, and you will be sons of the Most High, for he is kind to the ungrateful and the evil.

1 John 3:1

See what kind of love the Father has given to us, that we should be called children of God; and so we are. The reason why the world does not know us is that it did not know Him.

1 Corinthians 13:4-7

Love is patient and kind; love does not envy or boast; it is not arrogant or rude. It does not insist on its own way; it is not irritable or resentful; it does not rejoice at wrongdoing, but rejoices with the truth. Love bears all things, believes all things, hopes all things, endures all things.

Romans 13:8

Owe no one anything, except to love each other, for the one who loves another has fulfilled the law.

Romans 12:10

Love one another with brotherly affection. Outdo one another in showing honor.

Inspirational Verses about Having Faith

Matthew 21:21-22

And Jesus answered them, "Truly, I say to you, if you have faith and do not doubt, you will not only do what has been done to the fig tree, but even if you say to this mountain, 'Be taken up and thrown into the sea,' it will happen. And whatever you ask in prayer, you will receive, if you have faith."

Romans 10:17

So faith comes from hearing, and hearing through the word of Christ.

Hebrews 11:6

And without faith it is impossible to please Him, for whoever would draw near to God must believe that he exists and that he rewards those who seek Him.

Hebrews 11:1

Now faith is the assurance of things hoped for, the conviction of things not seen.

Mark 11:22-24

And Jesus answered them, "Have faith in God. Truly, I say to you, whoever says to this mountain, 'Be taken up and thrown into the sea,' and does not doubt in his heart, but believes that what he says will come to pass, it will be done for him. Therefore I tell you, whatever you ask in prayer, believe that you have received it, and it will be yours.

James 2:19

You believe that God is one; you do well. Even the demons believe—and shudder!

Luke 1:37

For nothing will be impossible with God.

Ephesians 2:8-9

For by grace you have been saved through faith. And this is not your own doing; it is the gift of God, not a result of works, so that no one may boast.

Proverbs 3:5-6

Trust in the Lord with all your heart, and do not lean on your own understanding. In all your ways acknowledge Him, and he will make straight your paths.

2 Corinthians 5:7

For we walk by faith, not by sight.

1 Peter 1:8-9

Though you have not seen Him, you love Him. Though you do not now see Him, you believe in Him and rejoice with joy that is inexpressible and filled with glory, obtaining the outcome of your faith, the salvation of your souls.

Romans 15:32

So that by God's will I may come to you with joy and be refreshed in your company.

Colossians 1:11

May you be strengthened with all power, according to his glorious might, for all endurance and patience with joy,

Psalm 5:11

But let all who take refuge in you rejoice; let them ever sing for joy, and spread your protection over them, that those who love your name may exult in you.

Hebrews 12:2

Looking to Jesus, the founder and perfecter of our faith, who for the joy that was set before Him endured the cross, despising the shame, and is seated at the right hand of the throne of God.

Psalm 30:11

You have turned for me my mourning into dancing; you have loosed my sackcloth and clothed me with gladness,

1 Chronicles 16:27

Splendor and majesty are before Him; strength and joy are in His place.

Encouraging Scriptures for Depression

John 14:27

Peace I leave with you; my peace I give to you. Not as the world gives do I give to you. Let not your hearts be troubled, neither let them be afraid.

Romans 15:13

May the God of hope fill you with all joy and peace in believing, so that by the power of the Holy Spirit you may abound in hope.

Romans 12:12

Rejoice in hope, be patient in tribulation, be constant in prayer.

James 1:2

Count it all joy, my brothers, when you meet trials of various kinds,

Philippians 4:4

Rejoice in the Lord always; again I will say, Rejoice.

Galatians 5:22

But the fruit of the Spirit is love, joy, peace, patience, kindness, goodness, faithfulness,

John 16:24

Until now you have asked nothing in my name. Ask, and you will receive, that your joy may be full.

Proverbs 17:22

A joyful heart is good medicine, but a crushed spirit dries up the bones.

1 Peter 1:8

Though you have not seen Him, you love Him. Though you do not now see Him, you believe in Him and rejoice with joy that is inexpressible and filled with glory,

John 16:22

So also you have sorrow now, but I will see you again, and your hearts will rejoice, and no one will take your joy from you.

Psalm 118:24

This is the day that the Lord has made; let us rejoice and be glad in it.

Psalm 16:11

You make known to me the path of life; in your presence there is fullness of joy; at your right hand are pleasures forevermore.

John 15:11

These things I have spoken to you, that my joy may be in you, and that your joy may be full.

Psalm 30:5

For his anger is but for a moment, and His favor is for a lifetime. Weeping may tarry for the night, but joy comes with the morning.

Psalm 16:9

Therefore my heart is glad, and my whole being rejoices; my flesh also dwells secure.

Psalm 4:7

You have put more joy in my heart than they have when their grain and wine abound.

1 Thessalonians 5:16-18

Rejoice always, pray without ceasing, give thanks in all circumstances; for this is the will of God in Christ Jesus for you.

Proverbs 10:28

The hope of the righteous brings joy, but the expectation of the wicked will perish.

Isaiah 55:12

"For you shall go out in joy and be led forth in peace; the mountains and the hills before you shall break forth into singing, and all the trees of the field shall clap their hands.

Luke 15:10

Just so, I tell you, there is joy before the angels of God over one sinner who repents."

Contact Information

Vicki Yohe Ministries

Vicki Yohe Ministries
P.O. Box 84818
Baton Rouge, LA 70884

info@vickiyohe.org
615-500-2103

ENDNOTES

1   The United Pentecostal Church International, formed in 1945, is the world's largest Apostolic (Oneness) Pentecostal Christian denomination, headquartered in Weldon Spring, Missouri. https://en.wikipedia.org/wiki/United_Pentecostal_Church_International

2   The Hymn "Great is Thy Faithfulness" © 1923. Ren. 1951 Hope Publishing Co., Carol Stream, IL 60188, William Marion Runyan, Thomas Obediah Chisholm

3   JMMI (Joshua Media Ministries International) Founded by David E. Taylor, incorporated in the State of Missouri in 2007, has several crusades across the country and was labeled a "cult" by many prominent Evangelical Christian leaders

4   "Rev. Jim Jones," born, James Warren Jones, was a religious cult leader who had 918 followers commit suicide by cyanide in 1978. https://en.wikipedia.org/wiki/Jim_Jones

5   "CDC - Fact Sheets-Alcohol Use & Health - Alcohol." Centers for Disease Control and Prevention, 3 Jan. 2018

6   Meryl Streep, famed Oscar-winning actress, also known for her advocacy for women's rights

7   Harvey Weinstein, is an American former film producer who abused his power to coerce and rape women. He was convicted, February 2020. https://en.wikipedia.org/wiki/Harvey_Weinstein

8   The Western Wall, "Wailing Wall," is an ancient limestone wall in the Old City of Jerusalem. It has also been called the "Wailing Wall", referring to the practice of Jews weeping at the site over the destruction of the temples. https://en.wikipedia.org/wiki/Western_Wall

9   Haman is the main antagonist in the Book of Esther, who, according to the Hebrew Bible, devised a plot to kill Jewish people. https://en.wikipedia.org/wiki/Haman

10   Christian Louboutin is a French fashion designer whose high-end stiletto footwear incorporates shiny, red-lacquered soles that have become his signature. https://en.wikipedia.org/wiki/Christian_Louboutin

11   "Dangerous Cult Leaders," Joe Navarro. https://www.jnforensics.com/post/dangerous-cult-leaders

12   Narcissism and Personality Disorders. "20 Signs of Toxic and Manipulative Men." https://divorcedmoms.com/20-signs-he-is-a-toxic-and-manipulative-men/

CPSIA information can be obtained
at www.ICGtesting.com
Printed in the USA
LVHW081254020420
652008LV00023B/3535